What Black Politicians Are Saying

WHAT BLACK POLITICIANS ARE SAYING

Edited by Nathan Wright, Jr.

Introduction by Julian Bond

HAWTHORN BOOKS, INC.

Publishers • New York

Dedicated appreciatively
to
the Black political leaders of the 1970's,
who will give new humane redirection
to the nation,
to
the Black President whom the 1970's will elect,
and to
the Black martyrs who inevitably must dramatize the
CAUSE OF FREEDOM

PREFACE

by Nathan Wright, Jr.

What these distinguished Black politicians are saying will be of tremendous importance for America, particularly during the next critical decade.

We are faced with a cultural revolution and a people's revolution. Both revolutions are related and both are political in nature. The cultural revolution is claiming the right of people to be or to become themselves in every sense of the word. Either America will accept this cultural revolution and become truly pluralistic, or it will perish through inner turmoil, distrust and dissension.

The people's revolution is calling for a universal democracy and not at the lowest common denominator. Rather, such a universal democracy calls for the elitist possibilities in every human life to be developed and to share in the determination of our common destiny.

WHAT BLACK POLITICIANS ARE SAYING

The Black politician is most representative of these two revolutionary forces which are active in American life today. These revolutions must succeed if the nation's basic commitments are to find fulfillment.

Some may wish to debate whether Black politicians are the most authentic conservatives in respect to our nation's professed ideals or whether they are our most advanced revolutionaries. The difference to me is somewhat rhetorical. Yet there is a point at which conservatives must see that revolutionary change is in their self-interest. At the same time, advocates of revolution must always envisage the achievement of some shared dream or past commitment. Otherwise, the revolutionary simply seeks change for the sake of change, and the conservative, in a reactionary way, loses sight of and a hold onto the basic values he seeks to preserve.

The articles by the Black politicians in this volume speak convincingly of programs for Black political action and of the problems and possibilities which are involved. Behind these engaging discussions are the essentially cultural and human concerns which will be most determinative of America's future.

The Black politician is freed in a singular way from loyalty to repressive elements in our society. Primarily because of this, he is best equipped to provide the new leadership which realistically promises peace, integrity and the best possible life for all of our nation's citizens.

Without the kind of leadership which Black politicians uniquely can afford, the nation may well face an eclipse which dims the fortunes of our people and reduces our primacy among the nations of the world.

The Honorable *Julian Bond,* Georgia state represen-

PREFACE

tative and a pioneer spokesman against the Vietnam war, places the role of the Black politician in a national focus in the Introduction and sets forth in Chapter 10 a Black Southern strategy. Often spoken of as a Presidential possibility, Julian Bond was nominated for Vice-President at the 1968 Democratic national convention. He has become one of the most popular young political spokesmen in America.

Anna R. Langford is possibly the first woman to be elected alderman in Chicago, winning her seat undisputedly in 1971. A volunteer lawyer during the Southern civil-rights marches in the early 1960's, Mrs. Langford has brought to the Chicago scene a fearless crusading spirit. Her gripping story of how she " 'Whupped' the Tar Out of the Daley Machine" begins Part I of the book, which is entitled "Building a Base of Power."

California State Senator *Mervyn M. Dymally* tells in a lively way of the almost meteoric rise of California Blacks to political power in Chapter 2. His story is like an autobiography of a Black political giant. His emphasis upon Black organization and Black self-interest underscores his conviction that those who succeed in politics know how to speak to power with power or temporary interests which happen to coincide. Senator Dymally is editor of a new book, *The Black Politician: His Struggle for Power* (Belmont, California: Doxbury Press, 1971).

Dr. *Fannie Lou Hamer*, of the Ruleville, Mississippi, Freedom Democratic Party, of which she is a founder and vice-chairman, has brought Blacks and whites together in an unprecedented way. A "grassrootsy" woman with three honorary degrees, Mrs. Hamer explains in Chapter 3 how survival can be achieved in the South.

In August 1964 she led a delegation to Atlantic City, New Jersey, which won a pledge from the Democratic National Convention not to seat any future delegations that barred Blacks from membership.

In Chapter 4, *Jesse Jackson*, the "Mayor of Chicago's South Side," speaks with humor and religious insight of the need for Blacks to recognize that their religious heritage has been—and can continue to be—a source of power. The Reverend Jesse Jackson is the national executive of Operation Breadbasket, which spearheads economic opportunity for the Black masses. Jesse Jackson, like Julian Bond, is a compelling spokesman for a new political outreach and is one from whom the nation will hear much in the several decades which lie ahead.

Part II of the book focuses upon serving human needs, although the themes of each part of the book intertwine and are woven through the book. *Dick Gregory* in Chapter 5 uses the medium of humor to tell a devastating story of how we have failed as a people to eliminate poverty in spite of unprecedented wealth. He sees racism as far more than a joke which we have played upon ourselves and calls, in his inimitable way, for a moral regeneration in our total life. Mr. Gregory ran for President *on the issues* in 1968 and promises the possibility of a repeat performance. He is also author of *No More Lies: The Myth and Reality of American History* (New York: Harper & Row, 1971) and *Dick Gregory's Political Primer* (New York: Harper & Row, 1972).

The Honorable *Shirley Chisholm* is a former teacher and state legislator who bucked the local political machine and has been elected to Congress twice. Things have not been the same in Washington since her arrival. She has brought brilliance and dignity to her work and has added luster to the Congress. In Chapter 6 Mrs. Chisholm reveals the broad range of human concerns which have engaged her interest and which make her one of the most attractive public figures in America today. Mrs. Chisholm is author of *Unbought and Unbossed* (Boston: Houghton Mifflin Co., 1970).

In Chapter 7 Congressman *John Conyers, Jr.*, speaks of the global effects of entrenched racism in America. In his speaking out for African interests, he reflects a growing fraternity between Blacks of African descent throughout the world, despite some recent press comments to the contrary. John Conyers, Jr., has taken a leading role in organizing the Congressional Black Caucas. Himself a Presidential possibility for 1972 and 1976, Conyers places issues forward with persistence, directness and a statesmanlike sophistication. In Chapter 9 he sets forth a Black political strategy for 1972.

In Chapter 8 Mayor *Kenneth A. Gibson*, of Newark, New Jersey, goes to the heart of the human concerns which face our cities. He speaks of the need for organization, for new coalitions of business and community leaders in the cities and in their suburbs—and for national aid—if America's Newarks are to remain the vital force which they should be. A winsome, able and sometimes reserved leader, Kenneth Gibson has demonstrated how "revolutionary" elements may act politically to conserve the best in urban America.

Part III of the book contains four essays on "Black Strategies." In addition to the contributions by Julian

Bond and John Conyers, Jr., Percy Sutton and John
Logan Cashin speak from a national and a regional point
of view, respectively.

The Honorable *Percy Sutton,* Manhattan Borough
President, presents in Chapter 11 an extremely thoughtful piece on the technical subject of the communications
media as a necessity for future Black political power.
Mr. Sutton has been instrumental in accomplishing in
New York City much of the program which he recom-
mends in terms of Black control of their communities'
means of communication. Percy Sutton is the "Dean of
Black Elected Officials" and holds promise, as do the
other contributors, of a highly significant role on the
national political scene during the coming decade.

Dr. *John Logan Cashin* is a dentist and human dy-
namo from Huntsville, Alabama. He is the founder and
present chairman of the National Democratic Party
of Alabama, which represents authentically both Blacks
and whites in Alabama. The NDPA, as the party is
called, has challenged the Wallace machine with a remarkable show of strength. Dr. Cashin's article, "Challenging the White Bourbon Power Structure," Chapter
12, tells of how Blacks and whites may work together for
a new day in Southern politics.

Part IV of the book is entited "The Political Setting."
From the point of view of a social scientist, I have written Chapter 13, "The Social Arena of Black Political Action." The maze of human problems which seem
to crush us at this present point and to which the Black
politicians bring a ready resource are dealt with. There
is also a commentary upon the difficulties which our

governmental processes have placed in the path of new aspirants to political power and place.

Blacks bring to the nation's life today unique gifts which our public life needs for its revitalization and redirection. To look upon increased black leadership as an act of justice may be fair, but it misses the key point that, for the nation's greatest good, Blacks must quickly assume disproportionate roles of influence in public affairs. A Black man or woman for President must be only a beginning, if we are as a people to experience the depth of rehumanization required for us to realize the full measure of our nation's potential greatness.

CONTENTS

WHAT BLACK POLITICIANS ARE SAYING

CONTENTS

Part IV

The Political Setting

INTRODUCTION

by Julian Bond

In 1971 the National Urban Coalition tried to spell out what was wrong in this country and how it could be set right. "America's malaise," they said—which all of us feel in one way or another—"has its roots in the distance between national ideal and national reality.

"Our ideal is a country where every American gets an equal chance to perform, where jobs exist for everyone who wants one, where health care and personal safety are assured, where we live in harmony with each other and have a decent place to live.

"Our reality needs no full recital here. We know that the cities are in trouble, that poverty continues in the midst of wealth, that unemployment is high, that malnutrition is widespread, that injustice exists, that tensions endure. In sum, we know that our society is not functioning the way it is supposed to.

"But if we solve the greatest of our ills," the Coalition said, "our paralysis of spirit and will—we can narrow the distance between what we have and what we want. Indeed, we *must* marshal our good sense and our good will—there is no sensible alternative."

In the Coalition view, "America must pursue several major goals between now and 1976. It must try to:

"Achieve full employment with a high level of economic growth—all of our other policy goals depend upon it.

"Provide all citizens with an equal opportunity to participate in American society and in the shaping of governmental decisions affecting their lives.

"Guarantee that no American will go without the basic necessities: food, shelter, health care, a healthy environment, personal safety, and an adequate income.

"Meet our obligations to assist in the economic development of the world's lesser-developed nations.

"These are the goals. We can move a long way toward them by 1976." *

But in addition to the Coalition's major goals and their definition of "paralysis of will" as the greatest of our ills, there is another goal more desirable and another ill more horrible. The ill is racism and the goal is its containment and eradication.

It is redundant today for any American to tell any other American what is wrong with this country and what can be done to set it right.

Everyone knows, or ought to know, that there is one consuming problem that makes life in New York's Har-

*Unpublished draft, "Statement on National Priorities." The National Urban Coalition, January 18, 1971.

INTRODUCTION

lem, Cleveland's Hough, Los Angeles' Watts or Atlanta's
Vine City—or any of America's other Atticas where
some men are held in bondage by some other men—
both intolerable and insufferable.

That problem is race. It is race that elected our present President in 1968; race that makes housewives ugly
in Pontiac; race that makes some Americans serve and
die more readily than others in Vietnam; race that makes
some children more educated than others; race that is
making our cities wastelands.

For the past several years solutions to the problem
of race—and thus to the pathologies of society that
spring from it—have been more than abundant.

There are several solutions that, if implemented,
would begin to make this country a proper place for
men and women to live and work and a healthy place
for our children to play and grow and learn.

The nation can adopt, and strive for, a policy of full
employment.

Equal opportunity, both racially and sexually, can stop
being the rhetoric of campaigns and platforms and become the reality of the present.

Through public-service employment, increased economic growth, increases in wage minimums and in
minimum-wage coverage, and in guaranteeing social
insurance, radically altering public assistance, every
American can be guaranteed an income.

The institution of a national health insurance program and a radical alteration of federal housing programs will additionally aid in making both urban and
rural America more attractive places to live.

I have glossed over these solutions in order to get to

the means of financing them: through different federal budget priorities and a more equitable tax system.

For example, agricultural subsidies could be cut by $1.2 billion, while rural residents could be provided with expanded rural non-farm job opportunities.

Federal highway subsidies could be reduced by $1 billion a year, with the funds applied to the more urgent need of mass transit.

Other funds are obtainable by reducing expenditures for the Army Corps of Engineers (currently $1.4 billion) and Merchant Marine subsidies ($330 billion) and most importantly a cut in military spending of $30 billion by immediately withdrawing all advisers *and* military personnel from all of Southeast Asia.

None of these things will be done unless there is increased interest among the people in politics who desire these changes, unless there is a growth in political activism and organization beginning now and continuing throughout the rest of the decade.

This is a drive toward organization that must spring from a careful calculation of what is at stake and what the issues may be.

For some Americans, it may simply be an exchange of faces on a dormitory-wall dart board; for Black people, it is whether we progress, run in place, or continue sliding backward as we have been since 1968.

The purpose for which politically minded people must immediately organize now is to influence the selection, nomination and election of a new President, Vice-President and Congress in 1972.

On one level, the choice for the top office is simple: Anyone to the left of the incumbent will do.

On another, higher level, the nominee must be someone who delivers reality, not rhetoric, to the Black community.

It must be someone who will put teeth into the demands for a decent life.

Since the present President took office in January 1969, we have spent billions more on war, over two million more Americans have been added to the ranks of the unemployed, two and a half million more are on ever-mounting relief rolls, inflation has reduced our standard of living, and many American cities face bankruptcy. The racist policies of public and private U.S. institutions ensure that Blacks and other oppressed peoples suffer more than others, in good times and in bad.

The Vice-President's selection is less important but must be watched as well. Most importantly, it must not be one of the new crop of Dixie governors, these professional white Southerners who are like political nymphomaniacs, satiated only by the ultimate concession to their desires: a return to the illicit and incestuous political and personal relationships their ancestors enjoyed in the past. They like to hide behind the gratuitous Northern inclination to compare them to the worst of what we had before; they win easy congratulations for making statements on race in Georgia, South Carolina, and Florida that would start a riot in Harlem.

A new Congress will be chosen in 1972 also. These must for the most part be new men and women, not the tired old faces of the past. It must be a Congress that would reject the family destruction plan. That would have said *no* to more war, *no* to the continuation of starving children eating lead for dinner, *no* to freezes on wages with no freezes on profits, *no* to Reagan-Feller repression in America's concentration camps, *no* to J. Edgar Hoover's Federal Bureau of Intimidation, *no* to military millions for twentieth-century imperialism, *no* to Nixonomics and Mitchell's Mixups, *no* to the systematic destruction of Black people, our homes, our few jobs, our children, our very lives.

This seemingly magical transformation can be achieved.

It is not too soon to begin now. In fact, it is nearly too late. The process is difficult and easy at the same time. It involves involving yourself in politics, my profession, the second oldest profession in the world.

The first difficulty will be dealing with those who will tell you that politics is useless and accomplishes nothing. These are, incidentally, the same people who in 1968 would have told you that Richard Nixon's election was a good thing, because it would heighten the contradictions and hasten the revolution. That's fine in theory, but it's Black people's contradictions that are being heightened, not theirs. These are the spiritual descendants of the people who in Germany in the 1930's urged the election of Adolph Hitler for the same reason.

Politics is not the art of the possible, as we were taught in high-school civics, or even the art of the compromise, as many of us learned in Pol. Sci. 101, but a much more serious art: the art of seeing who gets how much of what from whom.

Black and poor Americans, of course, are the "who who haven't gotten any of anything from you know who."

There can then be no denying that the direction

INTRODUCTION

Black and poor people must take in the remainder of the 1970's is toward a real and meaningful participation in a new politics.

If there is anyone who believes it makes no difference who is President in this country, they should ask themselves these questions:

Who nominated Carswell and Haynesworth to the Supreme Court?

Who made John Mitchell the Attorney General of the United States?

Whose Department of Injustice tolerates murder at Attica, San Quentin, at Jackson State, at Orangeburg, at Kent State?

Who gave the Cinderella bridgegroom from South Carolina, Strom Thurmond, veto power over judicial appointees and school-integration decisions?

Whose Secretary of Defense says that the war against the Vietnamese people may end immediately, but American soldiers will be in Vietnam for many years to come?

Who is afraid of the hillbilly Hitler from Alabama?

Who was it who made the gate-mouthed Maryland farmer the Vice-President of the United States?

Who was that man?

It was the duly elected President of the United States.

And who were the people who let him do these things?

With some few exceptions, it was the Congress of the United States, the Representatives whose terms expire every two years and the Senators whose terms expire every six years.

WHAT BLACK POLITICIANS ARE SAYING

You should closely examine yours. They may be perfect men. If they are not, don't just check them out, kick them out.

I believe that Black politicians and political activists, as the only representatives of Black people selected in a democratic fashion from a base in the mass of the Black community across the country, had better begin as soon as possible to pull together a coherent strategy for 1972 and beyond. The August 1971 convening of the Southern Black caucus in Mobile, Alabama, which strongly urged Blacks to support no candidate, and the "secret" Chicago meeting of Black political activists is just a beginning of the sort of planning and coordination that must go on if we are to maximize our strength, increase our numbers and our power, and bring about some substantial changes in the lives of the people who look to us for leadership.

In 1968, out of a voting population of 120 million people, only 73 million voted. Richard Nixon received 31 million votes, but half again as many people, 47 million, did not vote at all. These statistics can be reversed and their result can be reversed.

It can be done, but it never will be done by people who think they can smoke America to her knees. It will not be done by a people whose major concern is macrobiotic diets, or music, or drugs, or the relative revisionism of the late Ho Chi Minh, or the romantic rhetoric of revolution, or the ennobling sacrifice of self-induced poverty, or if you enjoy Woodstock while you tolerate Watts, or if Boone's Farm or if bid whist is your major preoccupation, or if shouting "Off the pig" replaces the hard and dirty work of organizing the dispossessed into an effective force for change.

Remember, if this task is undertaken, some words from the past, from the great abolitionist Frederick Douglass, who said:

"If there is no struggle, there is no progress. Those who profess to favor freedom and yet deprecate agitation are men who want crops without plowing up the ground. They want the rain without thunder and lightning. They want the ocean without the awful roar of her mighty waters. The struggle may be a physical one, and it may be a moral one, or it may be both moral and physical, but there must be a struggle. Power concedes nothing without a demand. It never has, and it never will. . . ."

PART I
BUILDING A BASE
OF POWER

Chapter 1

HOW I "WHUPPED" *
THE TAR OUT OF THE
DALEY MACHINE

by Anna R. Langford

PERSISTENT OPPRESSION

Angela Y. Davis, in her brilliant lecture series at the University of California at Los Angeles in 1969, laid down a condition precedent for Black people if they are to dismantle the repressive political machines built by the Mayor Daleys of America and, in turn, build new citadels of freedom.

"The path toward freedom," wrote Sister Davis, "can only be envisioned by the slave when he actively rejects his chains. The first phase of liberation is the decision to reject the image of himself which the slave-owner has painted, to reject the conditions which the

* With affectionate apologies to a great Black man, Muhammad Ali.

3

slaveowner has created, to reject his own existence, to reject himself as slave."

In 1972, that historical imperative is as true of the Black peoples' struggle against the twentieth-century political plantation masters as it was in 1831 for our Black forefathers and mothers. The iron chains have been removed, but the chains on our minds and our souls are still there. An oppressed people are taught to accept their oppression, to internalize it, even to find ways in which it can be made respectable and almost enjoyable. The political plantation master of 1972 who keeps his darkies loyal to him by doling out small political favors and anointing HNICs ("Head Niggers in Charge") to act in his name is playing the same old "divide and conquer" game his forefathers experienced when they made some slaves "house servants" and kept the others out in the field.

I'm not much of an exception to the laws of history. Like most of my people, I've long accepted the values of our racist society. In many ways I've fought against those values, but I never confronted them. This is because I had never really rejected the image of myself which the political plantation masters had painted.

I have lived in Chicago for thirty years. In fact, a major part of my adult existence coincides with the last three terms of one of the most oppressive and racist political machines in the history of America—the Daley machine. For white people, Chicago Mayor Richard J. Daley had built a political machine which masquerades under the name of Cook County Democratic Organization. For Black people, this instrument has been a political plantation. That is the difference. And although I fought Mr. Daley's system in many ways—in the courts, in civic organizations and through civil-rights protests—I had never really confronted this terrible juggernaut with all of its awesome prerogatives that kept Black people segregated in housing, isolated in education and exploited in jobs.

No matter how terrible conditions became in Chicago—the construction of concrete concentration camps known as public housing, the murder of a Black alderman, the notoriously open buying of votes and the unashamed stealing of votes at elections—there was always a Daley-controlled Black lackey to pass out political goodies to "keep the natives quiet."

The average American simply doesn't understand the political tyranny that provides the oil for the Daley machine. If one word can sum up its methods, its operation and its philosophy, that word is *control.* Nothing in Chicago is done without Mayor Richard J. Daley's approval or blessing. Whether it's the settling of a teacher's strike, the construction of a new building, the appointment of a member of the Board of Education, the Board's election of its president, the employment of a nurse's aide in a county hospital, the selection of a Black man to run for Congress with the Democratic party's support, the manipulation of the City Council's entire legislative program, the granting of welfare assistance, the renting of a public-housing apartment, the conduct of the police force toward Black people, the granting of a license to open a business, the decision to repair which streets first, the awarding of garbage-collection contracts, none—not one, "nary a one"—of these things is done without the full involvement and approval of

5

the Daley political machine. Total control of the city for the benefit of the Daley machine to keep that machine in power sums up its primary purpose. Were Mayor Richard J. Daley to rewrite the ending of the Emancipator's famed Gettysburg Address, he would have no difficulty in substituting "that this government, of the machine, by the machine and for the machine, shall not perish from Chicago." A string of thousands of political casualties bears mute testimony to this sad fact of life.

I HAD TO RUN FOR OFFICE

I'm not sure what particular act of oppression or non-action of contempt for the people made me decide to run for alderman as an independent Democrat against the entrenched Democratic Daley machine of Chicago.

Maybe it's something like an illness which you live with and you keep thinking it's going to get better. So you never go to the doctor. Finally, you wake up one morning and one of the worst pains you have ever experienced is searing your body. At that point, almost too late, you go to the doctor and he quickly cures you. But you have lived with that sickness that has slowly destroyed your body. You have lived with it because, for any number of reasons, you just have not had time to go to the doctor or you were able to take some medicine to relieve a slight discomfort, or the pain just was not that intense and an earlier diagnosis several years ago had indicated that one day you might have to have an operation, but the prognosis was favorable for recovery with surgery. So you learn to live with your suffering.

As had many Chicago Blacks, I had learned to live with the disability of racism exemplified by the Daley machine. Then, one morning, I decided that I was not going to tolerate this worsened suffering any longer. The pain had to go.

And that is how I made my decision to run for alderman in Chicago. I woke up one morning and simply decided that the Daley machine, with its officious contempt for the poor, its disdain for the oppressed and its political manipulation of Black people, was no longer going to control my ward, my neighborhood, my street —at least not without my fighting the hell out of them on their own ground with their own rules and in their own game.

The 16th ward is typical of what is happening to all large cities in America. In fact, the 16th ward is a sociological microcosm of Chicago's inability—and the Daley machine's failure—to improve the living conditions of the poor and the Black. The 16th ward includes an area known as Englewood and part of West Englewood. The economic lifeblood of the ward is the Englewood shopping center, which dominates the 63rd–State–Halsted streets area. Several of the country's largest chain stores, specialty shops and supermarkets are located in the area. Its economics has been dominated by the Englewood Businessmen's Association and its politics has been dictated by the Daley political machine. This unobtrusive symbiosis has operated to the detriment of Black people.

Thirty years ago the 16th ward was predominantly

white. Englewood was a suburbanlike, tree-shaded community of single-family and two-family houses with carefully tended lawns. In search of the same good life sought by their white peers, Blacks began moving into Englewood. By 1960 it was 68.9 percent Black, its median family income for its 22,000 families $5,579 (fifteenth lowest of Chicago's seventy-five community areas), with only 26 percent of the families owning their own homes. The slide downward had slowly begun. By 1970, Englewood had become a virtually all-Black community with isolated pockets of stranded whites, too poor or too numb to flee.

When I first moved into the Englewood area, the garbage removal was efficient, the streets were kept clean and police protection was reasonably good. As the 16th ward became arithmetically Blacker, municipal services became geometrically inferior. Accelerating the decline of the area as a community of middle-class owner-occupied homes was the Englewood Businessmen's Association campaign to build the Halsted Mall, a modern shopping center. As welcomed an economic boost to the area as the Halsted Mall was supposed to have been, it also meant the loss of three hundred homes, the majority owned by Black families.

The Green Street Association, a local civic group, went to court in an effort to stop the demolition of these three hundred homes, and it was this campaign that enlisted the energies of the Reverend Dr. Martin Luther King, Jr., when he began his Chicago crusade in 1966. What Dr. King was soon to learn was that it was easier to effect more meaningful change for Black people on the Southern plantations controlled by the Sheriff Jim Clarks than on the Northern plantations controlled by the Mayor Richard Daleys.

By 1965, Englewood and the 16th ward were complexes of urban pathologies. Housing density tripled, dilapidated housing rapidly increased, police-Black community relations worsened as reports of police brutality were publicized and the schools turned into custodial jails for Black children. Nothing was done to meet the recreational needs of Black youngsters. With only one swimming pool in the entire area, it was a common sight to see Black children line up for blocks in 100-degree heat, waiting for one to two hours to get into the pool for twenty to twenty-five minutes so the next group could cool off briefly. This cruelty was matched by the fact that there was not (and still isn't) a single boys club in the area.

Englewood further distinguished itself with one of the highest school drop-out rates and one of the highest teen-age unemployment rates in the city.

To Paul Sheridan, who had ruled the 16th ward for twenty years as its alderman, the name of the game was politics as usual. Why bother to take care of your constituents when they would still vote for you no matter how callous your attitude was? Why bother to maintain essential municipal services for Blacks at the same level you did for whites when you knew that Blacks would vote for you solely because you were the Democratic machine candidate? Suddenly, that sickness I had been living with became too much to bear and I decided to run for alderman.

WHAT BLACK POLITICIANS ARE SAYING

THE RISKS OF RUNNING

Sheridan got wind up of my intentions and he approached me one day at a civic meeting. "I hear you're thinking about running for my aldermanic seat," he said.

"I am," I replied with my warmest smile.

He frowned slightly, as though this audaciousness didn't make any sense, and asked the next question: "Why?"

"Because I want to be alderman," I replied.

"But what do you really want?" he persisted with a still bewildered look.

"I want to be alderman," I repeated.

He relaxed his face and continued. "Do you need something or is there anything I can do to help you? Whatever it is, why don't you come around to my office and talk about it? I can help you and give you what you want."

I shook my head. "No, you cannot give me what I want."

"Well, what do you want? Tell me, I can take care of it."

I knew my answer would end the conversation. "I want to be alderman. You won't give me that."

Shortly after our encounter, Alderman Sheridan died. For two years, the 16th ward had no alderman. In short, a predominantly Black ward just wasn't worth political representation. There would be no special election. The niggers would just have to wait for two years (1967), when the next municipal election was scheduled. I knew it was mandatory for me to run.

The Daley machine pulled off a cute trick by slating Sheridan's son, Paul, Jr., as its candidate for alderman. After all, the name Sheridan had been magic all these years and brought home the political bacon (even after that bacon had changed from white votes to Black votes) without any special effort. It's typical of political machines that they never tamper with what they consider a successfully tested formula. Paul, Jr., had moved out of the ward, but that presented no problem. He simply moved into his mother's house in the ward to qualify for residency. (In the environs of the Daley-controlled Board of Elections, you can do just about anything you want—as long as you are a Daley loyalist. The machine protects you.)

I resented this demonstrable contempt for Black people and it made me more determined than ever to do something about the politics of Ward 16. I also believed that if I could win and beat the Daley machine, it might provide the impetus for Blacks all over the city finally to challenge the stranglehold the Daley plantation had maintained over our political independence.

Recognizing I was an unknown political quantity, I started out by distributing stickers which simply asked the question "Who is Ann Langford?" My son, Larry, Jr., and I walked all over the 16th ward plastering the stickers on every conceivable empty space. The psychological payoff for me came one day when I walked into a supermarket with one of the stickers on my briefcase. A man asked me if I knew who Ann Langford was.

WHAT BLACK POLITICIANS ARE SAYING

I smiled and told him that I was Ann Langford. He then wanted to know what the sticker meant. I explained it to him. He smiled in relief and said he had been pulling his hair out trying to find out something about this "Ann Langford" and was relieved to have the mystery explained. He smiled and said he might even vote for me. "We can't do any worse than what we've had in there so far," he said, laughing.

But as pleasant as such small incidents were, I knew they represented only the tip of the Chicago iceberg of machine domination. An independent political challenge in Chicago is a rarity. Not only is the Chicago electorate —both Black and white—accustomed to lining up like Pavlovian sheep and voting for the machine out of sheer conditioned habit and nothing else, but the whole electoral process is totally controlled by the Daley machine. The machine decides what judges are to be nominated for all of the courts, what officials are to be appointed and hired, what workers are to be assigned to the polls, whom the police are to protect and arrest for election violations, which precinct judges are to be assigned and how much money is to be allocated to each precinct to buy votes. The machinery is so designed as to protect the "ins" and to discourage independents from running. If through some freakish unexpectancy an independent does manage to get on the ballot, he or she then faces a series of court challenges and unbelievable harassments. A good example of the kind of brutal harassments an independent can experience was that of Fred Hubbard, who was shot during the 1966 Congressional campaign when he ran against Republican

BUILDING A BASE OF POWER

William L. Dawson, one of the vestigial powers of the Daley machine.

Aware of the oligarchial power of the Daley machine and the possibility of violence, I went about organizing my campaign with as much professional skill as I could muster. The first task was to acquire a base of operations. On 63rd Street, I finally came across a large dilapidated building which had originally been renovated to house a double store. Because the owners refused to rent, I ended up having to buy the building. There was inadequate heat, and as the November aldermanic elections approached, there were many evenings when my band of dedicated workers, young and old, sat through the meetings in coats, boots and gloves.

THE PUNISHMENT OF LOSING

I ran into the usual unanticipated problems that were caused more by Mother Nature than Father Daley. One of the worst snowstorms in the city's history brought all traffic to a standstill, and for four days I was unable to get my literature around to houses. The snowstorm also caused me difficulty in getting my literature printed and hampered my efforts to get special literature to the Spanish-speaking voters in the ward.

We knew we were infiltrated by spies from the Daley machine, but so many of our campaign tactics had a distinct amateurish cast to them and we were so strapped for funds that we figured the reports would promise very little likelihood of victory.

WHAT BLACK POLITICIANS ARE SAYING

Despite our lack of funds, our comparatively fewer campaign workers and the problems caused by the snowstorm, we compensated with innovations such as coffee sips all over the ward. I ended up drinking coffee in people's basements, living rooms and kitchens whenever a small group could be assembled. Several times I ran into Paul Sheridan, Jr., at these sips, and after a few short debates which quickly revealed to the groups what a political zero he was, he made it a point not to appear with me anymore.

Election day was an unhappy combination of our own mistakes and naïveté and the unbridled corruption of the Daley-controlled Democratic machine. We didn't have enough people to man the polling places. We made the mistake of putting poll watchers in the white precincts west of Ashland Street, which went so heavily for Sheridan that scrupulous observance by our people was a massive exercise in futility. It was the Black precincts where the vote-buying was heaviest and where the police were observed as bending over backward to be partial to the machine precinct captains that our presence was most needed. Votes were going for as much as $5 each. It's hard to match that kind of money with an already impoverished campaign budget.

But with all of the chicanery attempted by the Daley machine workers, Sheridan and I were still running neck and neck when the returns started coming in for the first twenty-eight precincts. (There are fifty-five precincts in the 16th ward.) Then, suddenly, everything stopped and there was no flow of information from any of the precincts. We called the newspapers, police headquarters and City Hall but were unable to learn anything for about two hours. Then, as suddenly as the returns had stopped, they began again, and this time they were coming in high for Sheridan and low for me. According to a source close to the political top, two sets of figures had been fed into police headquarters with a discrepancy of 2,000 votes in the second set called in.

One Black precinct in particular came in strong for Sheridan, a 200-vote margin. A post-election check revealed that the election was lost in this precinct.

Even more depressing was the fact that Sheridan— or rather the Daley machine—defeated me for a run-off in the end by only thirty-seven votes. Sheridan was proclaimed alderman by a mere thirty-seven-vote majority.

Naturally, we filed a petition for recount, charging among other fraudulent activities that particularly in the 200-vote-margin Black precinct our poll watchers had been intimidated by the police and Daley machine-controlled election judges, ballot applications had been altered (after the polls had closed), ballots were sorted by a police officer who simply threw them into piles and counted them without any election official supervision and then passed on the totals to the election judge, who accepted his verbal count without verification. I not only lost the case in the lower court, but the decision was upheld by both the Illinois appellate and supreme courts.

From then on, I was more than determined than ever to stake my claim to the 16th ward aldermanic seat. The white power structure, with its male oppressors, had held this seat too long. It was time for a Black woman to take it away from them and "bring it on back" to the Black community of self-determination and keep it there.*

There was one casualty of this campaign. My marriage. This unfortunate development demonstrates the extreme lengths to which the political machine will go to preserve its Neanderthalic power base. For years, my husband had been trying to get into police communications, a position reserved for a group of white occupational elitists. About six months after my election defeat, my husband joined the regular organization and he was subsequently and quickly given this job which he had sought so long in vain. Had my husband been a long-time political worker or activist, the machine's eager embrace of him would have made some political sense. But he had no record of political activity. The intent was obvious: to embarrass me in the event I did intend to carry out my threat and run again in 1971.

But there are times in all of our lives when some higher principle, some higher commitment, consumes us at the risk of our personal fortunes and demands a sacrifice to a cause which is not so much noble as it is simply humanitarian. No woman should be forced to choose between backing her husband and the destruc-

* Englewood Black youth, especially males, needed a strong, Black male image, having been too long exposed to the female-dominated home, school, and what have you. If a strong, independent Black man had run for alderman in 1967, I would gladly have supported him. But such was not the case. So, better a woman alderman who was independent of the machine than a Black man who would be selected and elected by the machine on the basis of his disposition to be bought and paid for by Massa Daley.

tion of political corruption. But if Black women, and any other women, make the complete riddance of the politically cancerous and racist Daley machines everywhere in America the main goals in their lives, Black people will high-jump to freedom instead of crawling on our stomachs, as we do now.

But these setbacks only strengthened me. I was determined to make my enemies my footstool. The day after my 1967 defeat, I began organizing for my 1971 victory.

REGROUPING FORCES

I remodeled the old building I had purchased, moved my office into it in 1969 and began practicing law from the neighborhood address. A large community room in the building was turned over to the neighborhood for meetings. I plunged into a diversity of school activities, including a trip to Washington, D.C., with one school group. A youth group was formed to assist me, and I began organizing every identifiable element in the community—laborers, ministers, housewives, teachers and gang members. We understood only one goal: unify to defeat the Daley machine.

At the same time, Operation Breadbasket had begun conducting classes in political action to train people as poll watchers, precinct organizers, election judges, drivers and voter-registration volunteers. Many of these persons were natural allies and were of immense help in my campaign.

In addition, I received considerable advice and encouragement from an old friend, former newsman and editor Wesley South, who hosted a popular radio show, "Hot Line," on soul-oriented WVON. Wesley kept me tuned into important issues, and there were times when some of his listeners must have believed that all Ann Langford did was call into "Hot Line," but this kept my name—and my voice—before the Black electorate.

I consistently took a strong militant position on most issues and of course found myself at odds with the Daley machine and its totally muzzled Black non-spokesmen. Because the Daley machine had been able to build its plantation by ignoring the urban crises facing the Black ghetto, it adopted a "business as usual" stance. They even helped my campaign by slating an unknown building inspector. But my machine-endorsed opponent was a nice quiet man who made little impression on the people whenever he appeared in public. Occasionally, when we were asked to be on television programs together, he would refuse, and I was able to hit consistently at his contempt for the voters.

There were also those occasions when the unexpected worked in my political favor, just as the unanticipated (the snowstorm in 1967) had sometimes worked against me. One day I happened to be in City Hall when hundreds of young people from two high schools showed up, demanding to see the Mayor to present him with 50,000 signatures calling for Warren Bacon, a Black member of the school board, to be named board president. (It was a widely accepted fact that Mayor Daley was instrumental in preventing the election of this dynamic and capable Black man to the school-board presidency.) The kids weren't permitted to get on the elevator, and a wall of helmeted police (the kids called them "Daley storm troopers") stood in front of them. I told the police I would get on the elevator with them and we would all be arrested, stating loudly at the same time that we would be arrested for getting on a public elevator in a public building. We were then permitted to go up to Mayor Daley's office, where the school kids met with one of Daley's aides, talked with him for about a half hour, then held a press conference. Later, they crowded around me, shaking my hands and thanking me for standing with them. "When you run for alderman, we're going to work for you," some of them shouted to me. And some of them did. It was a happy day for all of us.

But I have long felt that children are as important a part of the political process as their allegedly more intelligent elders. Toward this belief, I did try to educate the children in my neighborhood to political issues. Not only did I welcome them to visit me in my building whenever they felt inclined, but also I began the practice of bringing fruit from my Michigan farm to them. There was always in the fall season a supply of fresh apples waiting for them. Soon the office became a place for twenty to thirty children to gather during their lunch hour. These children, it appeared later, persuaded their parents to vote for me.

One week before the election day of February 23, I sent out a letter to all of the election judges (dated February 17) which set forth who I was, what I had done and what I expected from them. In one page I wrote, among other things, that "I expect an honest election due to the high morality of the judges in this ward and the recent prosecution of judges who have been guilty of fraud in election in other wards. However, I am prepared to detect and prosecute any acts of fraud which might escape your observation of February 23, 1971. I won this election once, and I do not intend to have it stolen from me again. Kindly pass this word on to others who gain access to the polls bent on winning this election by whatever means possible, short of getting the popular vote honestly."

In subsequent conversations with many of the judges, I learned that the letter definitely had an impact on their thinking and actions on election day.

I had one of the most faithful and dedicated volunteer staffs which, along with other notable effects, mailed out over 25,000 pieces of literature, saturating the 16th ward. Many of the women and teen-agers stayed up all night, addressing and licking envelopes. Those small, seemingly unimportant and drab jobs are the nuts and bolts of any election. Somebody has to run the errands, empty the wastebaskets, lick envelopes and make telephone calls. We had our share of these lovely, dedicated people. There were times when sheer exhaustion in the middle of the night forced us to put down records, relax with a few furious sessions of the "boogaloo" and the "Philly dog," then go back to work, physically more fatigued, but with our souls uplifted with that brief infusion of "soul." We are a swinging people.

ELECTION PROBLEMS

But political success comes only with hard work and shrewd anticipations of your opponent's next moves.

BUILDING A BASE OF POWER

The Daley machine's moves are easy to diagnose because they follow the dictates of Lord Acton's theory that "power tends to corrupt and absolute power corrupts absolutely." With its near absolute power over the fief of Chicago, the Daley machine could be expected to pursue its repressive tactics and, of course, it always did.

We were confident that the same corrupt practices would be repeated during the 1971 election, especially the manipulation of the ballot count. So we did two things. We recruited some of the toughest members of the neighborhood gangs we could find and enrolled them in classes on poll watching.* Next, we assigned two of the most alert from the group and sent them to the 27th precinct, where the election had been stolen from me. The two young men were "big, Black and beautiful." Well dressed, they were courteous, insistent and unfailingly polite.

Ballots arrive at the polling booths in sealed packages and, according to the rules, the judges can use a package only if it has an even 100 in it. The first package to be opened in the 27th precinct contained fewer than 100 ballots. The election judge proceeded to open a second package to make up the deficiency. Our young poll watcher told her not to do it that way but to close the first package and open another. She did so reluctantly and opened a third package, which had more than 100. She began to remove the excess number to put them aside in a separate pile (the opportunities for a

---

* They were all happy to participate in what was considered a respectable community endeavor inasmuch as they had usually been ignored and shut out of such activities.

fraudulent count are obvious in this kind of practice). Our poll watcher again told her to close that defective package. When the judge protested, he quietly pulled out his election rules book and read her the precise section that required her to follow his instructions. The election judge then opened next to the last ballot packages before she came to the one package with exactly 100 ballots in it. She then asked the young man what would have happened if none had had an even 100 ballots in it. He replied they would have had to send out for some more packages or nobody would have voted! This reflective and quiet conclusion came from a gang member, mind you, a group which the press has painted as a so-called destructive force in our society. It should be noted that the fradulent count in the 27th precinct which had cost me the 1967 election was held down to almost zero, and this time only a few votes separated me and the machine candidate in that precinct. This feat was accomplished because of two beautiful, young Black dudes whose commitment to Black self-determination was made compatible with their desires to be members of a gang. It was a happy merger of mutual needs in the Black community in order to defeat the historical racism of the Daley machine.

If you weigh the assets against liabilities of my campaign, it's difficult to put one's finger on which assets were the most important to victory and which liabilities had to be minimized to achieve victory. My campaign was truly a collective effort.*

* For one thing, I had no official campaign manager. Everyone who seemed to exercise some kind of influence in a given area was my "campaign manager." Further, it was that person's

BUILDING A BASE OF POWER

I would, however, outline some of the liabilities which confronted us during the campaign and on election day. 1) Finances. We spent a total of $6,000, of which $3,000 was my own money. The Daley machine was reported to have spent over $25,000. 2) The poster fight. Our posters were constantly being torn down, and this tended to dismay my workers. I told them not to retaliate but simply to put my posters next to that of my opponent on fences and billboards. Posts and fences don't vote; people do. But to the average voter who is saturated with advertisements, posters and public announcements, such media saturation is equated with guaranteed victory. 3) The newspaper–Democratic organization coordination of effort. The Daley machine floated a number of unfavorable rumors about me, but the most damaging one that continued to surface was that I was a Republican. In a city which is 85 percent Democratic, that rumor alone can defeat you. The Chicago *Tribune* erroneously published the statement that I was a Republican and this tended to authenticate the rumor because it had appeared in the newspaper. It cost me some votes but not enough to defeat me. 4) The usual Daley-machine harassments, which were many but with which we had learned to live and cope. 5) Apathy. This factor has long been one of the most serious deterrents to the exercise of democracy in a democracy. Apathy has so forcefully influenced the electoral process —due to the preponderance of oligarchical control of the

---

responsibility to carry out an assignment without being interfered with or second-guessed. This tactic was very ego-building and resulted in that person giving his best to the campaign and delivering the votes expected of him or her.

election process—that we now speak about "grassroots democracy." Democracy itself should be grassroots, but the Boss Daleys, who are only the latest in a wretched legacy of political bosses from Boss Tweed, Boss Flynn, Boss Pendergrast to Boss Hague, Boss Roraback and Boss Curley, have corrupted the democratic process by trying to remake it in their own selfish image. In turn, people have been turned off by democracy and just don't bother to vote in primaries because they recognize that so many primaries are corrupt or have already been decided by the presentation to them of two pre-selected alternatives over which they have had no say. In the 1971 16th-ward aldermanic primary, only 29.9 percent of the registered voters voted. That figure alone indicts Chicago Mayor Richard J. Daley as a political boss who has done next to nothing to inspire political involvement of the masses.

PLUS FACTORS

The assets of a political campaign and subsequent election are the confluential determinants of victory. Mine were responsible for the ultimate triumph. 1) Total people involvement. The people ran my campaign. Different people had different skills and know-how. They were given assignments and they carried them out. There were about ten Ann Langford campaign managers! 2) Professional assistance. There were several top-level political, labor and business professionals who helped organize specific areas. John Swearingin, who is head of the post-office union, did a fantastic job as an organizer of people and resources. Leon Davis, administrative assistant to Congressman Ab Mikya, and Richard Barnett conducted classes on political education. Richard Stamz and George Murphy, who had long been involved in the 16th ward Regular Democratic organization, came into my office and were so impressed that they associated themselves with my campaign and lent the years of their organizational expertise and knowledge to many of our unsmooth and amateurish efforts. 3) The organizational belief that I didn't have a chance. Few people thought I could win, and certainly none of the vassals in the Daley barony believed me capable of upsetting this virtually unassailable pachyderm. The newspapers, taking their cue from the Daley machine, were silent about my candidacy, and whenever they did discuss the various women candidates, I was invariably omitted. One writer, Harry Golden, named the women he believed had a chance to win and excluded me. (There were ten women candidates in the races.) Many of my workers angrily called in wanting to protest, but I told them to let sleeping dogs lie. We would make Mr. Golden eat his words on election—and he did! 4) A hard-hitting, unrelenting campaign. I campaigned on one issue—getting off the Daley plantation, emancipating ourselves from his machine's stranglehold on Black progress. I called attention to all of the urban and racial ills that had existed in Englewood for the last eighteen years and that nobody had cared or done anything about them. I talked about payroll padding and actually gave examples of people being carried on the municipal payrolls while receiving up to $50,000 a year in salaries while practicing law on the side; about a clerk of the court who earned $28,000 while renting three trucks to the city for an annual rental of $25,000; about their $11,000 homes which they had bought years ago and were still unpaid for because of excessive real-estate taxes which soaked them but which favored big business in Chicago. All I had to do was to cite various newspaper articles which exposed the endemic corruption of the Daley machine—quoting from former crusading editor of the Chicago *Daily Defender*, Chuck Stone, who drove the Daley out of its mind until he was fired to the Chicago *Tribune*, a Daley machine ally which had exposed many corrupt practices such as ghost voters and non-voting residences. 5) A well-organized "truth and protective squad." I had hired three big, Black and—to use white folks' terminology—burly uniformed security guards, who traveled with me constantly on election day. With their badges, guns and uniforms, we encountered litte resistance in our demands to see evidences of all alleged fraud which were constantly being telephoned to me. My son, six feet one, with his motorcycle jacket and helmet, also accompanied me, and a newspaper photographer was the final but accidental member of the truth section of my squad. In one instance I had to confront an election judge at a polling place who had ejected my poll watchers after the polls closed. With my "truth and protective squad" accompanying me, I dashed over there and, with an angry finger waggling in the election judge's face, for the first time lost my cool, and as the brothers would say, I got very colored indeed. I told him that as hard as I had worked to win this election, I would knock his teeth down his "goddamned throat" if he tried to steal the election from me. My poll watcher was readmitted, the ballots were counted, and I carried that precinct. It was another case of internalizing both types of behavior characterized by Machiavelli in his classic *The Prince*: "A prince being thus obliged to know well how to act as a beast must imitate the fox and the lion, for the lion cannot protect himself from traps, nor the fox from wolves. One must therefore be a fox to recognize traps and a lion to frighten wolves." There has never been a more perfect description of the evils of the Daley machine—traps and wolves. Finally, 6) close liaison with all of the elements of law, order and justice in government who were natural enemies of the Daley machine. I maintained close touch with the state Attorney General's office (a Republican), and teams of lawyers from his office constantly accompanied me, checking out reported instances of fraudulent activities.

After the polls closed we began the long, anxiety-ridden wait. We had done everything we could think of. We had matched organizational skill for organizational skill, intimidation tactic for intimidation tactic, shrewdness for shrewdness. My workers had been instructed not to leave any polling place until the ballots were finally totaled and verified by a tally on the judge's sheet. Despite the fact that all but seven precincts reported had me leading by over 700 votes and I knew I had won, I refused to open any champagne bottles or permit any celebration until *all* the precincts were in and all the ballots were counted. (Remember Charles Evans Hughes, who went to bed in 1916 believing he had defeated Woodrow Wilson?)

WHAT BLACK POLITICIANS ARE SAYING

VICTORY . . . AT LAST

The Chicago *Tribune*, which has never in its entire history been a friend of the Black community, declared Mrs. Marilou McCarthy Hedlund of the 48th ward as the first woman to be elected to the City Council and that "Mrs. Langford claimed the lead in the 16th ward." By so doing, this enabled American society to preserve its precious white heritage by having a white woman as the first elected woman alderman, despite the fact that we both won on the same day. Whether Mrs. Hedlund or I won "first" is immaterial. It's like arguing which twin is older because one was born twenty minutes before the other one but on the same day!

The votes finally came in, and I had defeated my Daley machine-selected opponent 4,636 votes to 3,890 votes—a margin of 746 votes. (Mrs. Hedlund's margin of victory was 577 votes.)

We had done it, and once the figures were finally confirmed, then and only then did I permit all hell to break loose in my campaign headquarters, and as one sister phrased it two days later in her exhausted joy: "Honey, we carried on and partied like there was no tomorrow cuz our Black lady whupped Mr. Daley."

Yes, we "whupped" Mr. Daley and his machine. But "we" are only one ward. There are now fourteen Black aldermen out of fifty (28 percent). Using "Stone's Index of Proportionate Political Control" developed by Chuck Stone in his book *Black Political Power in America*, Blacks in Chicago still must elect four more Black aldermen for a total of eighteen in order to reflect the percentage of Blacks in the population. By the time the next election rolls around, however, in 1975, the Black population of Chicago will be 40 percent or more, which means we must start shooting for a total of twenty Black aldermen—and even more importantly, a strong, viable Black candidate for Mayor.

I exult in my "whupping" of the Daley machine not so much because it was a victory for Ann Langford but because it was an honest victory for a lot of hard-working and dedicated, politically sophisticated Black people who for years have teetered on the edge of political power but never before been responsible for change. This time, they—not Ann Langford—did it.

There were additional pluses and minuses accompanying my victory. A plus was the defection of large numbers of Black voters from the Daley plantation. In eleven Black wards—the 2nd, 3rd, 4th, 6th, 8th, 17th, 20th, 24th, 27th, 28th and 29th—the total vote for Mayor Daley (incidentally, he also was running for Mayor at the same time) dropped from 104,991 votes in 1963 and 103,616 votes in 1967 to only 72,237 votes in 1971.

So while Black voters in Chicago have not completely left the Daley plantation, at least they are beginning to boycott it!

This sharply decreasing Black vote also helped contribute to the lowest mayoral primary turnout in forty years—43.68 percent.

Secondly, a dismaying commentary on Black political sophistication was indicated by Black voters' decision not to follow the Reverend Jesse Jackson's endorsement of Daley's Republican opponent, Richard Friedman, who campaigned hard for the Black vote. It has been demonstrated repeatedly during the last sixteen years that Mayor Daley is not the best mayor for the Black people. Yet Black people are so wedded to the household of the Democratic party that many of us are afraid to step outside for a little fresh air and vote Republican. Thus the average Black voter in America continues to vote for a Democratic racist over a Republican integrationist.

As a Democrat, I by no means suggest that the Republicans are any more committed to helping Blacks than whites. As Congressman Clay of St. Louis has said, we have no permanent friends or permanent parties, only permanent interests. As long as the Republican party is controlled by some of the worst political Neanderthals represented by the Nixons, the Agnews and the Mitchells, Blacks have no alternative but to vote Democratic—or form their own party. But when a dedicated and proven civil-rights leader of the accomplishments and sacrifices of a Reverend Jesse Jackson urges Blacks to vote for a particular candidate and we ignore him, then we have an awful, an awful lot of political educating of Black folks to do.

As I look back on the campaign and examine the successes and the hurts, I would do it all over again, even if I knew it was going to come out the way it did. For example, my marriage. My husband aligned himself with the organization, indicating he had no choice if he wanted to keep his job. This is the kind of terrible thing machine politics does to people. Fortunately, my loyal son, Larry, Jr., hung in there with me, and his support was a source of comfort and security during some anxious moments.

What makes us run for political office? I don't think Black political aspirants will always write political history because of greedy, unconscionable and racist politicians who believe it is more important to pave their white pockets through graft, favors and patronage than to pave Black pockets of poverty with jobs, housing and education.

Ann Langford is only one member of a needed national Black crusade to "whup" other racist and repressive Daley machines throughout this country. When we can come together to achieve this goal, then and only then can America truly call itself "the land of the free and the home of the brave."

Chapter 2

THE RISE OF BLACK POLITICAL LEADERSHIP IN CALIFORNIA

by Mervyn M. Dymally

Ten years ago California Blacks were virtually im-
potent in the state political arena. Today the situation is
quite different. During the 1971 session of the California
legislature, for example, a Black senator held two key
committee chairmanships: chairman of the Senate Majority Caucus and chairman of the Elections and Reapportionment Committee. And 1971 was the crucial year
of reapportionment.

In the lower house of the California legislature,
Blacks also play vital roles in the leadership structure.
During the 1971 session of the Assembly there was a
Black chairman of the Ways and Means Committee, a
position second in importance only to the Speaker of the
Assembly. Furthermore, Black Assemblymen held the
important chairmanships in Urban Development and

Housing, Government Organization and Manpower Development. In the 1970 Assembly, the Democratic floor leader was Black.

The leadership positions held by California's Black state legislators illustrate the dramatic rise to power of a new generation of political activists—all within the decade of the 1960's. As the fruits of this early groundwork grow to ripening, those who have watched the development and refinement of Black political sophistication in California find no surprises even in two exciting recent successes: on Dellums' election to Congress and Wilson Riles's election as State Superintendent of Public Instruction.

Political plums of this type were bound to grow out of the intensive involvement of Blacks in the political process. In California, Blacks represent not only Black districts but some also hold statewide office or represent mostly white constituencies. In addition, Blacks have influenced the structure of the present State Central Committee and are some of the key supporters of its present chairman, Charles Manatt.

WHITE LIBERAL ARROGANCE

Though the flowering of Black political power in California started to come into view in the early 1970's, one must go back to the early 1960's to find the roots of that development. The new structuring of Black political power began with the advent of the Kennedy movement. Not that the Kennedy movement was so democratic. But it created excitement. Actually, the Kennedy campaign

33

was instituted around the same old racial stereotype that had plagued Blacks in the past: that Blacks needed to be coordinated by some white Ivy League student on leave of absence because we couldn't make decisions.

But the call for political action by the civil-rights activists during the 1950's and early 1960's brought a new dimension to Black aspirations within white-dominated political movements and it led, ultimately, to a new dimension of Black autonomy in the political participation of the 1960's. Thus, when the Kennedy movement hit the West Coast, young, dynamic Blacks sought to put these experiences into practical political play by joining the Young Democrats and the community groups for Kennedy in order to be involved in an organizational framework. The entire Black delegation of the Los Angeles City Council today started with Kennedy before they held office.

Then, as now, white liberals did not see the need for deliberately selecting Blacks in leadership roles. As a result of these paternalistic attitudes, the majority of Blacks in the Young Democrats found themselves in the moderate, rather than the liberal, camp of the young Democrats. The white liberals took it for granted, as they had over the years, that whites could and would represent Blacks properly. This was symptomatic of the white liberal disease of those days: They could not admit that they were unwilling to share power with Blacks. They also needed desperately to believe that they could do an even better job for Blacks than Blacks could do for themselves. The healthy and vigorous efforts of the new breed of Black politicians have helped reduce if not eliminate the symptoms of this disease.

BUILDING A BASE OF POWER

From their experiences in the Young Democrats, the young Blacks in the movement learned some valuable lessons that were to come in handy later on when they made their own bids for elective office. They learned many practical political maneuvers: how to caucus, how to bluff, how to count, how to finesse the opposition. They also learned how to evaluate the behavior of their "friends" more objectively. For example, it soon became clear that white liberals in the early 1960's in California were likely *not* to select Blacks for leadership positions, mostly because it would interfere with the ambitions of the whites themselves. There are many examples of this. It is significant that not one Black was ever appointed to a leadership position while Jess Unruh was Speaker of the California Assembly. A more recent example is the 1970 election in California. Pat Brown, Jr., son of former Democratic Governor Edmund G. Brown, pre-empted the office of Secretary of State by injecting himself into the race early in the campaign. At the same time that Brown was hoping his famous name would keep others from challenging him, the Republicans, to show they were not racist, were running a Black attorney, James Flournoy. If Brown had not followed the typical white-liberal pattern of refusing to relinquish power, Californians in 1970 would have had the interesting option of voting for either a Black Republican or a Black Democrat. With two Blacks pitted against each other for the office of Secretary of State, "race" would have dissipated as an issue and there would now be a Black Secretary of State. Instead, in a year in which every other statewide partisan office was won by the Republicans, only Flournoy was a loser. But, in reality, all California Blacks were the losers while another white liberal rode on to victory.

This is not a reflection on Brown, but it simply serves to focus on the problem: How can we get liberals to recognize the need for minority leadership?

ORGANIZING OURSELVES

Ironically, it was with the moderates rather than the liberals that some of the more effective coalitions could be worked out. The moderates labored hard to erase the stigma of "racist" from their identity. The liberals were arrogantly complacent.

It is worth noting that the California Democratic Council was ten years old before it had a Black on its executive committee. And it is one of the most "liberal" of all Democratic clubs.

The Blacks in the Young Democrats made a good record of forming coalitions to extend their influence. Blacks held various leadership positions with the Young Democrats and were supported in their bids for power by the moderate wing of the Young Democrats. One person was elected State Treasurer, another lost in his race for the State Presidency by only sixty-eight votes, and still another served as a member of the State Central Committee.

Having seen that politics could provide a forum to expose the issues, Blacks began to run for the legislature. This was not an easy road, for politics, prior to 1960, was an unexplored avenue in the Black community. Although the middle class was well organized in such groups as the National Association for the Advancement of Colored People, the Urban League and the Southern Christian Leadership Conference, there was no national or local movement in politics *per se*. Despite the absence of effective political organization in the past, some of the Blacks in the Young Democrats were successful in their initial bids for the State Assembly or the Los Angeles City Council. This is really quite a remarkable story in itself since the key to political success is *organization*. On the other hand, the Blacks who are now in top leadership positions do not regard their record of successful organizing as anything particularly surprising. In a recent article in which they were asked to explain the reasons for their high degree of success, every person interviewed cited skill at organizing as a major factor.* Typical of the reactions is that of Assemblyman Willie Brown, powerful chairman of the Assembly Ways and Means Committee, who said: "The positions held by Black legislators are in direct relationship to their individual and collective skill at in-house politics. It is certainly not the result of a desire by the white legislators to demonstrate that they are O.K. on the race issue. It is, rather, a reflection of our ability to stick together and move for each other unselfishly." In those early years in the state legislature, Blacks faced frustrating experiences. It has already been noted that Jess Unruh, leader of the Assembly Democrats and closely associated with both John and Robert Kennedy,

* Melvin Steinfield, "The Leadership Role of California Black Legislators," *The Black Politician: A Quarterly Journal of Current Political Thought*, Vol. 3, No. 1, July 1971, Urban Affairs Institute.

refused to promote a single Black to a leadership position. Only after Unruh lost power through his defeat for Governor in 1970 were Blacks able to assert themselves and move forward rapidly in leadership positions.

Another cause of frustration was the low expectation for the role of Blacks that was held by whites in the Assembly. Whites in general expected that the Blacks would be merely average and would be content to "stay in their place." Whenever there were any signs of getting "uppity," in terms of leadership aspirations, Blacks were stymied at every turn. This was, in a sense, a replay of earlier games that had been played in American history, both in the North and the South. Another frustration was discovering the conservative nature of the legislative process. Originally thought of as an institution to bring about radical change, it was soon discovered that the legislature, *and those who influence it,* are strong defenders of the *status quo.*

So the Blacks began to organize. They soon established such organizations as the California Conference of Black Elected Officials, which snowballed into the Western Conference of Black Elected Officials and eventually the National Conference of Black Elected Officials. Out of the National Conference emerged the Urban Affairs Institute and the Joint Center for Political Studies, as well as *The Black Politician,* a quarterly.

REPRESENTING HUMAN NEEDS

There were, of course, benefits to being a Black state legislator even though the state was not revolutionized in the process. For one thing, the legislature provided resources that normally were not available outside the legislature: staff, communication aids, use of media, contacts with various influential individuals and organizations. People began to pay closer attention to what these individuals had to say because now they were elected officials with some power. Serving in the legislature was therefore not without its benefits, but merely serving, without leadership influence, was not as productive as it could have been.

A final frustration was the realization that the Black elected official has a much harder row to hoe than his white counterpart for at least three reasons.

1) Few Blacks represent any economic special-interest group such as the oil interest, insurance, or the highway monopoly. The Black elected official represents *people*, mostly poor, minority and discriminated against. His interests are centered on *human* values, not *economic* interest.

2) He does not have available to him the economic resources that his white counterpart in the legislature has. White legislators receive ten times the amount of financial support for their election campaigns that Black officials do.

3) The demands by the constituent community are greater. The presence of the legislator in the district is vital. Legislation lacks visibility and the substitute is your presence in greater proportion than your white counterpart. When a bill is passed here, few Blacks see or feel the direct impact of it or are aware of its source.

Thus, the Black elected official must constantly make appearances to reassure the disenfranchised and the disillusioned that if we work together we can make changes through the system.

In my own particular case, it took the Watts riot to make me realize how deeply alienated from the legislative process most of my constituents were. They were alienated not only from the legislative process but from the "system."

The Watts riot was an unpredicted phenomenon. No one knew it would have taken the form and shape it did. But I was present when the first fire was lit at the corner of Central and Imperial, and I saw the behavior of police officers who panicked over very little at the time. On my suggestion that they cool it, one officer said that if I made one step he'd shoot. I said, "*Shoot, mother-fucker!*" I did this because I was caught in the emotion of the scene and didn't care. Now you can imagine just how deeply rooted and yet close to the surface the Black rage is if a state legislator with an important stake in society could reach the point of saying to a police officer with a gun pointed at his belly, "Shoot, motherfucker!"

After the riot, more people knew me because I received a lot of press. It was a very emotional time and under ordinary circumstances I would not do or say some of the things I said then. One suggestion I made when the press interviewed me at the time was: "Talk to all the indigenous leaders, including the Muslims." That statement was regarded as controversial enough to get a lot of publicity which taught me that, in the system we are operating under, *to get press you have to be controversial.* This showed that a Black politician could play a useful role in organizing the community as a spokesman for the oppressed.

BUILDING A BASE OF POWER

A BLACK AGENDA

My election to the state senate in the aftermath of the Watts riots and my outspoken comments to the press put into perspective the way I began to view the role of the Black politician. I came to a number of conclusions about the agenda for Black political leadership in California that may be relevant to national politics:

1) The role of the Black politician is to be an advocate of the people. *All the people!* Even if he does not share the views of the Panthers or the Muslims, he has an obligation to articulate the frustrations which are felt in the Black community.

2) The Black politician must recognize that rhetoric and mere symbolism do not necessarily produce meaningful change. We need to move far beyond the use of office primarily as a forum. We need to capture control of vital leadership positions. This is best achieved not via a third party but a third force. Black politics can become the focal point for a third force within the major party structures. We need to seek power, individually and collectively. And we must not be ashamed to state our objectives. Let the word go out that power is our tool, and justice is our commitment.

3) We must begin to develop young leadership not just in the elective positions but also in the key administrative positions. In California, the Deputy Director of Finance actually drafts the budget and is a Civil Service employee, unlike the Director of Finance, who is a political appointment. Directors of Finance come and go, but Deputy Directors last forever and survive

41

the defeat of many Governors. Blacks have to gain power in this area also. In California we have already developed a program whereby young Blacks serve an internship with elected officials.

4) In organizing for political power, we must avoid the kind of misguided democracy that feels an obligation to share all strategy secrets in public. Sometimes this type of all-inclusive revelation can lead to self-destruction. Once a press conference led to the denial of a grant. The Civilian Patrol in Los Angeles held a press conference just before they were scheduled to receive a federal grant. When a representative was asked what would be done if police solicited their support to apprehend a suspect, the reply was that they would not help the police. This answer was blown up by a conservative U.S. Senator and the grant was denied. We must learn from these mistakes of the past to avoid revealing more than is judicious for our needs.

5) The key to success is organization. Organization is hard work and requires many sacrifices. Once I was in England for a weekend conference when I received word of an important breakfast meeting of the Young Turks in the senate. The purpose was strategy and organization. I flew back just to attend that meeting, much to the dismay of my wife. But those are the essential details that need to be covered if we are to continue to stay on top of significant trends. It is the little details that add up.

6) We must assess the power we exercise realistically and objectively. The increase in Black mayors across the country is neutralized by the decay of the cities. What kind of power do we think we gain if it is a dead

city whose leadership we capture? For these reasons, and in view of the rise of Black political leadership in California, it is not out of order to suggest that we must now set our sights on the highest leadership positions in the state and nation. No longer can we afford to tailor our aspirations to the arbitrary expectations and guidelines of our "friends" and advisers. *We are our own best advisers.* For we are successful political practitioners as well as political scientists and we have passed tests that our white colleagues never had to take. Though the rise of Black political leadership in California has been meteoric, we can still do much better. I believe we can reach the stars. But first we have to aim.

Chapter 3

IF THE NAME OF THE GAME IS SURVIVE, SURVIVE

by Fannie Lou Hamer

I expect a drastic change to occur in this country, particularly in the Deep South, as Blacks become more aware of the importance of entering into politics and developing the skills necessary to find the solutions to the problems of "mass confusion." I believe there will be more interest generated in politics at the grassroots level by the everyday kind of people who have lost confidence in the democratic process because of corrupt politicians and their desire to perpetuate themselves in office while causing the masses to suffer.

MILITANCY IS NEEDED

I would not advise Blacks in the South to migrate to the North to change their situation. As a believer in

44

BUILDING A BASE OF POWER

God, I keep struggling with the belief that the situation in the South *can* and *must* be changed as more and more Blacks become registered voters. As more and more Blacks become registered voters, the old-line white racist politician will begin to feel uncomfortable. He will feel threatened at the thought of Black Power.

I consider the state of Georgia to be the most advanced in the area of politics. Here we have a Deep Southern state with more black members in its state legislature than there are blacks in the United States Congress. Too many of the so-called liberal Northern states are second to the state of Georgia, particularly the city of Atlanta, Georgia. However, in my opinion, race relations in the Deep South have not improved to any great degree. Just a short time ago in the state of Mississippi, a young high-school girl who was attending a white high school in Drew, Mississippi, was shot down as she stood looking at her hard-earned diploma of a few hours after graduation. She was a child who completed the first step toward the American way of "survival." Of course, I agree in general with the late Martin Luther King's "non-violent approach," but there are times when one has to take a more militant approach.

The new militancy on the part of Blacks and many young whites has caused not only the Deep South but also the North to realize that racism is an unnecessary evil which must be dealt with either by "men and governments" or by "men and guns." If survival is to be the name of the game, then men and governments must not move just to postpone violent confrontations but seek ways and means of channeling legitimate discontent into creative and progressive action for change.

45

WHAT BLACK POLITICIANS ARE SAYING

Politics will occupy the attention of the nation in the 1970's as the Black man makes his re-entry into the political arena. Step by step, the Black man will achieve many victories as we have seen in our Northern big cities. While this is important, I believe that the key to real progress and the survival of all men, not just the Black men, must begin at the local and country levels of government. While politics will not cure all of our ills, it is the first step toward electing a representative and a responsive government that will deal with basic human needs such as the right of all men to live decently and to have full access to unlimited opportunity

SHARED LOCAL CONTROL

Land, too, is important in the 1970's and beyond, as we move toward our ultimate goal of total freedom. Because of my belief in land reform, I have taken steps for acquiring land through cooperative ownership. In this manner, no individual has title to or complete use of the land. The concept of *total individual ownership* of huge acreages of land, by individuals, is at the base of our struggle for survival. In order for any people or nation to survive, land is necessary. However, individual ownership of land should not exceed the amount necessary to make a living in one's home, farm, or business. Cooperative ownership of land opens the door to many opportunities for group development of economic enterprises which build up the total community rather than create agencies which monopolize the resources of a community.

BUILDING A BASE OF POWER

Community living and group decision-making are what I mean by local self-government. It is this type of community self-government that has been lost over the decades and thus created decay in our rural areas in the South and in our Northern ghettoes. This is what we have seen played back to us time and time again, first as peaceful demonstrations and most recently in the form of violence and riots. If this nation is to survive, we must return to the concept of local self-government with everyone participating to the maximum degree possible. This is not to say, however, that we should not have a strong national or federal government, because these branches too must be responsive to the needs of all local and state governments through true representation of men and women who have *total commitment* to a true *democratic process*.

BLACK LEADERSHIP

As the Black politician returns to the scene of politics from years of deprivation he must restore the democratic principles of shared local control and responsiveness to human need. The "white racist politician," in his effort to control the minds of the Blacks and poor communities, has lost these principles. It seems to me that the salvation of this nation rests in the hands of the Almighty God and in the hands of the *Black striving politician* attempting to save his people and thus free the world.

Economically the Black community is crippled, mainly because of the lack of capital. The Black community does not have access to small business loans, local credits from banks in any sufficient amount and/ or private or individual grants. This is due solely to the fact that the Black community has been powerless and not only not represented but in many instances misrepresented. If the Black community is to thrive economically, there must be more unity and responsive leadership by the Black appointed and elected officials. I have high hope for the young people of this nation, both Black and white, because I believe that they are concerned. They are concerned that their children live free from the grandfather clause which says in effect unless your grandfather was rich and powerful, you must be a slave to the grandsons of those who were powerful.

WHITE HELP

In the near future the South will be a much better place in which to live than any place in the North. There is already a move on the part of the Blacks who migrated to the North during the "milk and honey era" to return to the South. Many of these Blacks have acquired professional and technical training which will be a great asset to the Black community as it seeks to develop economically. Of course the economic development of the South will also depend largely upon the speed with which honest communication in race relations develops. The Black community must depend to a large degree on the white community and the presently established institutions for the resources necessary to establish

Black-community-based business enterprises. The white community must see this development as an attempt to put the Black man on his feet. For example, several Blacks have recently demanded large sums of money from the white churches. This demand was called the "Black Manifesto," which in essence says that the church owes captial to Black development for use as seed money. The church for hundreds of years has collected these large sums of money and used them for literally nothing of human value. Hopefully, some of the demands will be met. As this economic development is taking place, Black economic leadership must be created. The Black community must have trained economic heroes as it has Black political heroes. They must have the vision to plan ahead for ten to twenty years at a time so that as the Black community grows, its economic enterprises will also be adequate. But until communication and race relations improve and the total community becomes united, we shall not see a significant change in the South. However, at the rate race relations and community life are improving, many of us will be long gone before substantial progress in this area has been made.

WORKING TOGETHER

As did Dr. Martin Luther King, I too have a dream that one day our children will live together, both Black and white, and not be ashamed to look each other in the face as human beings. God has blessed the Black man to endure more than three hundred years of suffering and today the Black man stands at the crossroads of the greatest period in American history. He stands not as a slave but as a man claiming full rights to all privileges which this nation has to offer, having made his contribution to every stage of development that this country has had. The history of this present period will record those valuable contributions, those successes and those failures and, yes, our struggle to survive.

Chapter 4

THE NEW SPIRIT OF '76

by Jesse Jackson

In 1776 a revolution took place because people were being abused. One of the phrases was called "taxation without representation." Some say that constitutes tyranny and that people who are subject to tyranny have a God-given right to rebel. They say that God does not mean for a man with a mouth to have to be quiet, that God does not mean for a man six feet tall to have to walk in situations where he can only stand five feet high. God does not mean for a man who has the brain potential to be a genius to have to settle for being a fool. So when he is trapped in a society that perverts his person, it is God who calls him to revolt. So in 1776, because of an abusive stamp tax and a tea tax imposed by absentee landlords, a group of people rebelled and created a revolution. Some may have referred to it as the "Spirit of 1776." Yet a revolution took place. Strangely enough, it was just a material revolution in one sense—in the sense that the American white and the Black who were involved revolted against being colonized but they did not revolt against colonialism. They broke up being colonized by Britain. Then they commenced to colonize their brothers at home. So it was half of a revolution.

POSTPONED PROMISE

In 1866, ninety years later, shortly after the Civil War had ended, there was an economic thrust launched that dealt with securing small portions of land. That year Congress passed the Southern Homestead Act. To show the marriage of economics and politics, Congress passed the act but the act was economic. That opened up public lands in slave areas—Alabama, Florida, Georgia and Louisiana—for the small farmers, for Black farmers. This was one of the first of the Reconstruction victories: getting land. Now, everybody cannot call for land. A dense man cannot call for land. A drunk man cannot call for land. An insensitive man cannot call for land because he cannot appreciate it. If his thoughts are cloudy with smoke, and if he is under the illusion created by dope, then he does not have the power to conquer the land.

If that man comes from the land, there has to be a kinship and we need to define the kinship between man and land. Both are forms of energy. A scripture writer tried to describe it by saying that man comes from the dust. When a man dies, no matter how metallic the caskets are, he still returns to dust. Some men when they leave the land do more with the land than others. Land is unconscious energy. Man is conscious energy. But both are forms of energy. If a man uses his brain he can conquer the land. A man with a clean brain and a clear mind will look at what an ignorant man might call greasy water, but he will see oil. Because his consciousness allows him to perceive what the unconscious man cannot see. A conscious man will see what most of us call trees but his consciousness also will allow him to see lumber.

Some men in 1866 who were not on dope, who had not lost the sense of the African tradition, came out of slavery fighting for land. Even without public schools, they were conscious. Even without airplanes and two-car garages, even without master's degrees they were conscious. A man conscious of the laws of nature and the universe is lost in no land. A man who is not conscious of the laws of the universe but who has chosen a narrow way will ultimately be engulfed by that land.

A group of new Black voters came after Reconstruction. They elected a number of Black legislators. The white folks didn't mind having a Black governor in Louisiana for forty days. It was what he was talking about that they objected to. White folks don't mind, even now, having thirteen Black Congressmen in Congress. If some of them are not going to support welfare legislation, they will let you have a hundred and thirty. It is the quality of their conversation that is going to determine the reaction. It was the plan of the Reconstruction Congressmen and politicians that created the reaction. White folks do not mind having Black politicians as long as they represent a white point of view. The Black politicians set up in 1866 a land grant. Eighty acres was the limit. Congress refused to pass this. And in 1876 they repealed the Homestead Act.

Presently, we are four years away from 1976. There's going to be some great celebrations. White folk have announced it on the TV and radio, calling it the "Spirit of '76." In Philadelphia, some man has been chosen to receive $85,000 a year from now until 1976 as the chief organizer of the "Spirit of 1976." Some of us may assume that the "Spirit of 1976" is going to be rooted in parade and in red, white and blue ornaments. But something is going down in 1976 that was the object of the first revolution. That revolution was to get land. This one is to maintain land. The "Spirit of 1976" may mean running Blacks back out of the inner city. We don't know. The "Spirit of 1976" may mean, because of technology, because of the protest of Black people, because of our international significance, because of the economics of uselessness that comes out of the computer, that in 1976 we do not need any Black people anymore. It may say that Black people are no longer necessary.

I don't know what it means, but there is evidence that white folks for 1976 have a plan. If they have a plan and we do not have a plan, we will develop a plan by default that is a reaction to their plan. The genius of the Southern civil-rights movement—in Montgomery, in Birmingham and in Selma—is that it represented actions initiated by Blacks which forced white America to react. The tragedy of the subsequent years is that it was the actions by whitey that made us react to them.

BUILDING A BASE OF POWER

We have an obligation to have our program in order, starting right now, for 1976. Of course, we realize that Black folks are in too much of a dilemma to appreciate entirely all that is involved in a good plan. In New Orleans, for example, where we have the Creoles, skin color is a great thing among us, but it's the same thing by different names everyplace else. All of us are kind of trapped between where we come from and where we are.

THE NEW VISION

I go to campuses all across this nation. While many students are not being shot in the arm with heroin, they are being shot in the head with misinformation. They fight to get in school what they could get free at home on the corner. There is a rage going now for Black history. I appreciate it. It is good basically for psychological self-esteem. It is good to know that we are a part of a great history and that we are links in and extensions of it. Yet the bleached bones and the great memories of our Black legacy will not feed us and clothe us and develop us. So while we need a Black history we must analyze a Black present. But even more time has got to be spent on the Black future. You can recall Black history and memorize it. But you've got to think out the analysis of the Black present. And you've got to envision the Black future. Thinking about today and envisioning tomorrow are far more challenging than memorizing yesterday. We are raised between civilizations. We've got African roots and we must not deny them. The fact is, however, we don't, as Black people in America, know what we are. We are something of a new people—neither African nor American—just a new people.

It may be that we were sent here by God to save the human race. Maybe the creative leadership and the soul and the sense of decency have come from this Black remnant, and the prophetic message for peace and justice has come from this community. Since it is the Black protest that has saved America from going absolutely crazy on the whole world, maybe it was Providence, rather than accidents, that held those ships up that allowed us to make it here under those inhuman conditions. Maybe it was not our government but our God who has sustained us. Hence, we need to integrate into our political and economic thrust a theology that puts God in His proper place.

A Godless people is a hopeless people. The emphasis of religion is a belief that life makes sense. If you do not believe that life makes sense, you are not going to register to vote. If you do not believe that life makes sense, you are not going to vote either. If you do not believe that life makes sense, then getting doped up does not matter. It is religion that breaks open the councils of despair and creates pillars out of lions' thighs and brings forth music from the growls they make. It is religion that takes the heat out of fire. It was that something—the Black man's religion—that the white writer could not describe, and Black writers were not sensitive enough to pick up on, that has led to such a terrible misinterpretation of these last fifteen years.

I went to Africa not long ago in order to have some of my beliefs confirmed. Africans love us. Sensitive

Africans realize that we are brothers. Many of them now have museums depicting the slave trade. But they have been so pulled apart that they are too weak to help themselves. It is sad but true that Ghana cannot go next door to help Nigeria. Nigeria cannot go next door to help Guinea. Neither of them can go east to help Kenya or Tanzania or Botswana. None of them are about to go south to deal with South Africa.

Given that reality, there is no danger of any Black brothers in Africa coming to Detroit, Chicago, New Orleans to save us. But the one consolation that I received (and I did get some consolation) was that we no longer see our black African brothers as savages subjected to the mysteries of Tarzan and Jane. Because some imagery has been cleared up, there is a new attitude of reflection in their voices and in their conversation. I would urge that Africa help us if Africa could. Africa would if Africa could. America could if America would. But since Africa cannot help and America is not going to help, we must stand up and fight for ourselves. No one is going to give us anything. I guess I am speaking about escapism, about grass looking greener. Without vision we will perish. Freedom is in the mind.

One needs perspective from the mountaintop in order to see the Promised Land. It is only from the mountaintop—that is, from a lofty, clear perspective—that you can ever see what the Promised Land affords. What is in the promised land? Hope. Opportunity. Food. Mutual respect. Jobs and income. This is beyond the mountain. Most of us are still in the valley. From the valley you can see the side of the mountain. And on this side of the mountain, you can only see its rough sides. That is why you hear the voices of despair talking about how soon the world is going to come to an end—how Black people cannot make it—God is dead—how powerful the bombs are—there is no salvation—"What y'all still marching for?"—"Ain't no change come." These are voices—valley voices—looking at the rough side of the mountain. From the mountaintop people discuss living out the true meaning of brotherhood, the highest possible relationship that human beings can achieve.

From 1955 to 1965 what I saw I saw as a boy in South Carolina. "Cause when y'all started in '55," I was in the eighth grade in Greensville, South Carolina. This is significant. Because the movement that Sister Coretta and Brother Martin gave leadership to has begun to produce a new human being. Walter Fauntroy, Julian Bond and John Lewis are also new evidences of something that broke in '55. Any man who has ever lived in the country knows something about ponds, where the fish are. When you throw the rock in the water, the ripples disturb the fish and they are not fast to bite because they sense that danger is near. In '55 the same God that once spoke to the jawbone of an ass, ironically spoke, using the voice of pain, through the toe of a woman and directed her to a prophet named Martin who threw a rock in the water—a giant rock in the water. Subsequent to that time, subsequent to '55, the SNCCs, the Panthers and the Malcolms and the caucuses and the mayors of the cities and the young Black leaders and whoever exists—these have all come about, the result of the ripple from the giant rock. There is one thing about history that the white man cannot create; that is an eraser that can erase the origin of that history. That rock is already in the water. Nobody can produce an eraser for history. You are lucky to be a ripple. But you are a fool to try to erase the place where the rock landed.

WHERE WE ONCE WERE

I am a reaction to and a product of a voice I heard on Spring Street one day in Greenville when I asked the question, "Daddy, why must we go to the back of the bus?" "Shut up, boy." I asked my daddy's friend, who was a boxer, a strong man, "Why do we go to the back of the bus?" "Don't worry about it, boy. Back of the bus getting where the front going. Besides, you ought to want to be with your own people. The blacker the berry, the sweeter the juice." Now, every once in a while we would want to sit near the front of the bus. Some of us remember our mothers snatching us by the arm, saying, "Come on, boy." It was because they were trapped in fear.

Then I heard a strange voice saying something like, "Walk together, children." Before voices in the South had the courage to talk, and before voices in the North had the sense to talk, there was a boy, come across WFBC on Spring Street one day, saying, "Walk together, children. Don't you get weary." And it went on to say that it is better 'cause I heard somebody say that I wouldn't mind walking. I might get tired. The voice answered again by saying it is better if you walk in dignity than ride in shame. So the water began to part. The rock indeed had cried out. Perhaps here is where we first found the Lord. Some thought that we left the South, the place where things first began to happen for us, but we didn't.

There was a period from 1955 to 1965 where we dramatized our intense humiliation. Humiliation: go to the back of the bus even though you pay the same fare. Humiliation: no public parks or libraries you can use even though you pay taxes. Humiliation: upstairs in movies. Back doors in hotels and cafés. Fancy hotels we now take for granted. But in our recent history we still had to come through the back door of a big hotel looking for a handout. Humiliation: all white police with no police warrants who were so absolute in their power until they were called "the law." In the South they did not even refer to them as police. That was a Northern term. They were "the law." This was just since 1955. An all-white judicial system in the midst of some of us going to school, majoring in political science, studying juridical ideas! Government of the people, for the people, by the people. Yet when we saw the judgment in action, the fear created in the humiliation was such that we saw but we did not see. Humiliation: a dual school system. Black teachers and white teachers working the same hours, only the Black teachers taught more students and taught double shifts and received less pay, still just within these few years.

At Sullivan Street School in Greenville we used books exactly three years after white students used them. We used desks exactly four years after whites used them. There were no Black school-board members. No Black members on the budget committee. No Black members on the planning committee. No Blacks building the schools that we were required to attend. We were rewarded for docility and punished for expressing personhood. Closed housing. Closed schools. Closed jobs. Closed conversations (talked up under our breath). Closed churches. Closed graveyards. Men called boys. Women called girls. We called white children "Master" and "Missy."

Within fifteen years: humiliation. I remember too well on the weekends at home when the gambling masters were running the skin games. The law would go around every Saturday afternoon, kick down doors and break up the skin game, take off the moonshine and the bootlegged liquor, lock up the men and herd them in the back of cars as their families watched them rolled away. But then on Monday they would put striped suits on those men and put chains on their legs and bring them back in front of their houses where their children and their wives could see them demeaned. I see friends of mine now, slipping chewing gum and cigarettes to their daddy, throwing them in the gutter so that when their daddy got to the gutter with the shovel, the daddy could pick up the cigarettes as if he had found them.

And the Black community, before the rock hit the water, was so unconscious that it was not even sensitive enough to get mad. It did not even make us mad. We laughed at the man with the chains on his ankles. Within fifteen years. You don't see it being written anywhere yet. So many jealous intellectuals who were not involved in action had chosen to use their pens and their boards as personal platforms to express their own guilt! And so the true story has not been told. This was a system of segregation.

In 1971, while we got the freedom to cuss, some of us spoke of separation. You may choose separation over and against integration, but there was no choice in segregation. Segregation was a legal system where you were forced apart for exploitation by law. You didn't choose whether you were to be segregated or not. You didn't have the choice to say, "I want to go to the Roosevelt-Fairmount Hotel," and say, "No, I believe I'll go to Holiday Inn," or "No, I believe I just want to be with the brothers in the ghetto." That set of choices does not exist in segregation. This period of humiliation witnessed a classic relationship between slave and master. It was bad that slaves were in the slums, but by this time, a hundred years later, the slums had gotten into the slaves. It was bad that we were treated as inferiors, but by this time we had begun to believe that we were inferior. We began to behave in an inferior manner. Our expectations of ourselves were low.

We figured that if we got a job making thirty dollars a week we were lucky. Our expectation was inferior. We figured if our neighbor's child went to school, to college, he was lucky. Our expectation was inferior. We did not even expect enough of God. We did not expect much of God. Our expectation was inferior. If God gave us a shack, that was better than somebody else's tent. We thanked him and quit working. We did not ask God for a house with two garages. We did not ask God for a livable income. In the labor movement, they were still fighting for a minimum wage. God would expect you to have a livable wage. And that is the difference. We did not ask God for any houses by the lake.

We did not ask God to thrive. We asked him to survive. We did not even expect much of God. Our whole picture of ourselves was inferior. When the prophet came, my personal position is, what he does has been misread by historians, as well as by many of us. When he was set apart and given his choice of divine offices, Moses' job was to save Pharaoh. "Let my people go." That was Moses' job. Our challenge has been for the people to let Pharaoh go. Pharaoh's not holding on to us.

FREEING OURSELVES OF PHARAOH

Pharaoh's not bothering us now, for the most part. Pharaoh has called us nigger, called us boy, called us girl. We build a white bank and a Black bank. We cannot make you turn Pharaoh's banker loose. White business and Black businesses—we cannot make you turn Pharaoh loose. Pharaoh runs to suburbs and then tries to possess land of the inner city. We ran past the land in the ghetto, going for the problem of the suburbs.

Our problem isn't that Pharaoh is holding us. It's us. We will not let Pharaoh go. We have developed a sense of dependence upon Pharaoh. We want to imitate him— his features, his hair style, his life style. We named our children after him. We needed his stamp of approval. He chose leaders for us. He told us what was right and what was wrong. We did not want Black music. We did not want the Black church. We did not want Black doctors. We did not want Black lawyers. We did not want Black judges. We did not want Black mayors. They were forced upon us. And we are trying in some cities now to throw them away.

We made excuses for Pharaoh's unregenerate evil. We made excuses for his beastly conduct. Sometimes we wanted to socialize with him when we should have been hospitalizing him. Sometimes we called him mean when we should have called him insane. Sometimes we reacted to him when we should have ignored him.

But the prophet led us on a mission. It was a mission to recover ourselves, not land. How are we going to get land if we haven't got the man? All the new talk about how we are going to take the ghetto! We are going to take over a state. We are going to take over a nation. But the rub is some people do not realize that "Nation Time" is a ripple off the rock that said it was "Man Time," that for Black folks it was "Somebody Time." Our first job for the first ten years, from 1955 to 1965, from Montgomery to Selma, was not to get the man but to get ourselves. We did not want to take away the white man's dignity. We wanted to get our own. We did not want to take away his respect. We wanted to get our own.

We had to be disciplined, and we had to suffer. And this is where some Northern reactionaries began to capture the white press, because they said, "Look at Martin Luther King, Abernathy, SCLC leading the people into further suffering." Many of them were on dope, and they did not understand that we were suffering. But the flow of the suffering had changed. We suffered in the cotton fields. We suffered building the railroads. We suffered being on the chain gang. We suffered not being able to use public accommodations. We suffered on the bus boycott. We suffered in Birmingham. But what was the difference? In the cotton fields and on the chain gang we suffered for the man. But in Montgomery and Selma we suffered for ourselves. That was the difference. Martin Luther King said that to live is to suffer, but to survive is to find meaning in the suffering. It does not make any sense that a man who knows the right of self still doesn't know a why for living. If you know why you are suffering, you can endure in a measure of suffering. If you know why you are somewhere, you can endure the heat of being there.

On the bloody Southern fields of struggle from 1955 to 1965, sweet things were visualized. Our minds matured. We captured more of ourselves. We began to experience the Kingdom of God in us rather than in white standards. Our demands for hope and liberation were in proportion to our mind's development. A man sitting in the back of a bus hands over the same fare. But if he demands the front seat, he may next demand to drive the bus. If he drives the bus, he may demand to get in the union. If he gets in the union, he may demand the right to own the bus company. If he demands the right to own the bus company, next he wants to go into politics so that he can enact laws to protect his economic investment. So it is, in fifteen years, that we went from the back of the bus to the potential political control of half of the major cities. But we did it logically. How are you going to ask to run for mayor when you haven't asked to sit at the front of the bus? It is not logical.

Dr. King used to talk about a freak in Greek mythology. Do not ask me any questions about Zeus other than this example he used to give about one mythological freak named Zeus. He said what makes Zeus a freak is that Zeus was born full-grown. He was born grown! He missed a relationship with his mother. He missed being a baby, a child and adolescent, a teen-ager. He grew without reason. He grew with no development. Zeus became worthy of a fool. He was not logical. God would not give me more than I can think. Nor would he deny what I am ready for.

Our movement, prophetically inspired, has been logical. One of the great tragedies of new young Black rebels is that their understanding is devoid of this kind of interpretation of the last fifteen years. Devoid of this understanding, they do not make errors that we made in the 1950's. Rather, they make errors of the nineteenth century.

In the nineteenth century, we failed to enter into the Promised Land because we had no clear collective sense of what we were called by God to be, as healers of this sick nation in which we suffer from the effects of its disease. Slavery took away our ambition and cruel oppression. Men who behaved like beasts made us believe that we, too, were less than men.

Our problem has been for too long a time that we have had no ambition. Nor have we possessed a sense of self which gives redemptive meaning and which enables us to go to the mountaintops and to look and then to move over into the Promised Land.

Today, a new revolution by Black folks is called for. Some might wish to call it the "Spirit of 1976." Whatever it is called, it will make a time of Jubilee, when things are set out in the way God intended them to be. Because of the mountaintop years in which the recent prophets led us on our way, Black folks now may hope to occupy their land and control their own lives. So may America become what it should be, and we as Black people stand united with our Black brothers throughout the world.

PART II
SERVING HUMAN NEEDS

Chapter 5

FROM POVERTY
TO PRESIDENT

by Dick Gregory

Even though this is supposed to be a book about "what Black politicians are saying," if you white readers really want to have some fun, you should come with me to the Black ghetto and hear how the white candidates campaign in our neighborhood. They behave entirely different in Black neighborhoods than they do in white neighborhoods.

For example, in the white neighborhoods, in the suburbs, a candidate comes riding in a limousine. That same white candidate comes into the Black neighborhood, in the ghetto, riding a mule . . . that's pulling a wagonload of watermelon!

When the white candidate is campaigning in the suburbs, he or she is always picking up some little babies to kiss. Of course, the white candidate also kisses babies in the Black ghetto. The only difference is that the candidate wears a surgical mask!

And in the suburbs, the white candidate comes out clearly against busing. In the Black ghetto, the candidate can't make a switch and be in favor of busing, because there are too many members of the press around. So the candidate does little subtle things to get the idea across—like wearing a campaign button that reads "Go Greyhound."

Finally, in the suburbs, the white male candidate talks about his war exploits. He'll make a speech on how he single-handedly won World War II. But in the Black ghetto he tells how he was stranded in the desert during World War II, bleeding, parched and starving to death, when a Black soldier fought off nine thousand Nazis to come to his aid. He tells how the Black soldier took out his razor and cut up his own shirt to make bandages for him. Then he tells of being nursed back to health with the only things the Black soldier had to use—a pint of gin and five pounds of chitlins!

Ever since I was a Presidential candidate in 1968, it's really strange how I get involved in politics, even though I don't intend to. On April 24, 1971, at a peace rally in San Francisco, I announced that I would not take another bite of solid food until the war is over in Vietnam. And while I've been on this fast, I've been doing a lot of running to keep in shape. I run three, five, sometimes ten miles every day.

And since I travel around the country so much, I receive invitations to run with many celebrities who are also interested in track. For instance, when I was in California, Roosevelt Grier invited me to run with him.

Bill Cosby invited me to run with him. In Chicago, Muhammed Ali invited me to run with him. And Senator Muskie invited me *not* to run with him.

Of course, I understand that Senator Muskie is really regretting that statement he made that a Black would not be able to win on a national ticket in 1972. And he is really trying to apologize to us Black folks in certain little ways. For example, when he campaigns in the ghetto, he wears a natural wig.

But in all seriousness, it is ironic that *because* of Senator Muskie's statement, it is now more possible for a Black to win on a national ticket. The idea of a Black man or woman on a national ticket has been implanted in the minds of folks all over the country. And they hear President Nixon, Vice-President Agnew, Senator Humphrey and others reacting to the statement by Senator Muskie, saying that *of course* in America anyone should be considered a candidate regardless of race or religious affiliation. Senator Muskie's statement has forced some very high-level backing for a Black candidacy, and folks all over America find themselves seriously considering the issue for the first time.

It is much like John F. Kennedy's candidacy in 1960. There was much talk that it was not possible for a Roman Catholic to win on a national ticket. The then Senator Kennedy said that he was entering the West Virginia primary to prove that it *was* possible for a Roman Catholic to be supported by the American electorate. Voters who had not even thought about the issue before were put to the test, and the rest is history.

But white politicians make some strange statements At the time of this writing, the Democrats are saying,

WHAT BLACK POLITICIANS ARE SAYING

"If President Nixon goes to the People's Republic of China in 1972, it will enhance his political chances of being re-elected." That statement just goes to show how dumb some Democrats are. They don't seem to realize that the way Nixon has messed up the economy in this country he could meet with God in 1972 and not be re-elected.

There is no doubt about the fact that the money *is bad*. I never realized how bad the money situation was in America until I got on an airplane the other day and a white cat sitting next to me said, "I sure would like to borrow some money, but the interest rate is too high."

I said, "How much is it?"

"Six percent," the white cat answered.

I was really shocked and said, "When did it get so low?"

We Black folks have always been used to high interest rates. I remember in 1969 they charged me 63 percent on a Motorola television set—with no knobs on it. I called the company to complain. "If I don't get some knobs on my set by next week, I'm gonna send my set back." And the cat on the other end of the phone informed me that if I didn't make my next payment by noon, they'd take care of getting that set back!

It's always been amusing to me to hear older folks talking about "the good old days." Now it looks like President Nixon is bringing back "the good old days" and nobody wants them. I hear white folks crying and complaining that it looks like the country is headed into another depression. I tell them, "You white folks might be, but we Black folks never came out of the last one."

I remember those "good old days" only *too well*. Like

so many other Black folks, I came from a large family. There were so many of us kids sleeping in one bed that if I got up to go to the bathroom during the night I'd have to leave a bookmark so I wouldn't lose my spot. Our family was so large that once a year my father would pack us up and take us all out to dinner and it would cost him $125. And that was at a 10-cent hamburger stand.

And, of course, like all large Black families we were poor. I remember one time I was uptight for money, so I went to my father and said, "Dad, if you don't give me a nickel I'm going to run away from home." He looked at me and said, "I'm not going to give you one damn penny, and take your brothers with you." Our family was so poor that even poor folks talked about us. One time we even got garnished by the newspaper boy.

Being so poor, we never had enough food. My mama used to want me to join the Boy Scouts. "I want you to join the Boy Scouts, Richard, and go to camp and learn how to rough it." And I used to tell her, "Mama, I want to learn how to 'rough it' like du Pont's boys! If you're really interested in kids learning how to 'rough it,' you ought to invite the Boys Scouts by our house. If the Boy Scouts think it's rough rubbing them sticks together and lighting a fire with no matches, let them try coming by here to eat dinner with no food."

I never will forget the Thanksgiving of 1942. My mama came home with a turkey foot. All of us kids gathered around the pot while Mama boiled the foot and we watched it shrink. Then we all sat around the table looking at that turkey foot and waiting to dive into it, and Mama insisted that we pray over it first. I said,

"Mama, I don't have anything against prayers or any-think like that. But if anyone should be praying, it should be the turkey that got away from that foot."

When I was a kid, Halloween was about the only holiday we could enjoy. Halloween was the one day we could wear our regular clothes and people thought we were dressed for the occasion. Folks would look at me and say, "Look at Richard wearing that old man's cos-tume. And he's wearing shoes that look just like feet." In my neighborhood, we kids couldn't play "trick or treat" like kids do in white neighborhoods. It was more like "trick and retreat."

And, of course, being a large, poor, Black family, we were on relief. One thing I could never understand is how so many Black folks seem to be ashamed of being on welfare. How can anyone be ashamed of some free money? My mama used to say she was ashamed of being on welfare. And I used to tell her, "Mama, you ain't on welfare, we kids are. That money's for us. Aid to Dependent Children—ADC. If you're ashamed of it, Mama, just give me my little piece of change right now."

Then Mama used to say, "It isn't the money so much as the way those social workers make you feel when they come around the house snooping to see if a man's been here." Now I just couldn't believe that! Those social workers had been to college and they couldn't be so ignorant that they could see that many kids and not know that a man's been around some-where! I used to tell Mama, "If those social workers can see this houseful of kids and not know that a man has been around, tell them we don't need the money.

Say we Black folks make money the same way we make babies."

That's one thing I'll never be able to understand about President Nixon. He has two cousins on welfare and he doesn't seem to want to do anything for them. The big difference between a white President and a Black President is that a Black President would never have some cousins on welfare that he wouldn't help out. Because the Black President knows there is no Secret Service that could protect you from your angry cousins!

But President Nixon doesn't help out his own cousins on relief and then turns right around and gives the Lockheed aircraft company a $250 million welfare check. Yet the President and some members of Congress seem to feel that poor Black folks on welfare should stop having all those "illegitimate" kids and learn to pick themselves up by their own bootstraps. When I heard about that $250 million loan, I sent the president of Lockheed a telegram and said, "Why don't you folks learn to pick yourselves up by your own landing gears?" Hell, Lockheed doesn't even have any illegitimate planes.

I get so sick and tired of hearing people bad-mouth poor folks and folks on welfare, as though a person's financial condition had anything to do with the really important things in life, like morality and ethics. White folks talking about the "Negro" family and how the daddy is absent and the family is dominated by the mama. I say, "Dammit, there ain't never been a man in the house." What difference does it make? Maybe white folks should get rid of all them daddies, get them out of the house, and see if they can create the moral strength poor, courageous Black folks have created.

77

WHAT BLACK POLITICIANS ARE SAYING

Black folks in Alabama have proved that. If having a mama at the head of the household gives Black folks the courage and determination to fight snake politicians like George Wallace, to put Black folks on the ballot and to keep on pushin' until those Black folks are elected, then maybe we ought to get rid of all the men in America.

Having a daddy in the home doesn't mean anything. LBJ had a daddy at home and look at all the vicious things he did while he was in office. Richard Nixon had a daddy at home and look what he's doing now. Hell, even Al Capone had a daddy at home! So don't *tell* me about those old mama-and-daddy complexes. Tell me about those good ethics and that pure moral commitment.

That is what's happening in the Black community today. There's a whole bunch of swinging nice folks sitting down with just one thing in mind—getting it together. There's not a lot of carrying on like you usually see at political gatherings. No paper streaming down from the walls, no noisy bands playing and people running around screaming and shouting political tunes. Just getting it together. And that is very, very important. Because once the people get it together, you can't get rid of them. You can wipe out the so-called leaders, but you can't do away with the people. When the people in any movement understand who they are and how important they are, then you've really got a movement.

The answer to the problems confronting America today is pure moral commitment. The young folks in America, young folks all over the world, have realized that. People talk about a generation gap. It's really a moral gap. Older folks lie to the young folks twenty-four hours a day, and then when the kids catch them in the lie the older folks say, "It's a generation gap."

Every problem confronting this country today was created by sick, slimy, degenerate politicians, and the only thing that is going to solve those problems is pure moral, ethical statesmanship ability. There is a big difference between politicians and statesmen. There's a big difference in the way politicians and statesmen approach solving problems. In a time of crisis, a politician flexes his muscle. But a statesman, in a time of crisis, flexes his mind.

Every problem in this country was created by man, which means those problems can be solved overnight if men and women are willing to make some sacrifices. And making those sacrifices will take you through some changes for a while. The first time I went on a forty-day fast I weighed 280 pounds when I started and 95 pounds when I came off. Of course I went through some changes. But I didn't give in and when I came off the fast I was the boss.

Fasting has taught me a lot about commitment and sacrifice. If folks really want to make some changes in this American system, they've got to get on the moral track and make some sacrifices. They've got to give up some time. They've got to stop trying to "be cool," sitting around sipping cocktails and talking a game. They've got to get that bad alcohol out of their systems which does nothing but put you to sleep. There's no way in the world you can change a sick, degenerate system with alcohol in your body, putting your mind to sleep and polluting your own system. If alcohol could help make a change in the system, the Man would have placed it on the moon where Black folks couldn't get to it.

Many people have got to take some days off work to get out and organize. Many people have got to take some nights off to get out and see to it that folks are registered to vote. They can't be making excuses. "Oh, Black folks just won't vote." No, baby, this stinking, trampy white system has put Black folks to sleep for four hundred years. Black folks aren't just going to wake up all of a sudden just because we want them to. Committed folks have got to go out and start waking them up.

When a man trips or gets knocked down and falls in the gutter, he's not going to get up just because you show up with a clean suit and some knowledge. You've got to learn how to bend down and lift him out of that gutter without getting down in the gutter yourself.

The people and their moral commitment will decide the fate and destiny of this country. It's a big job. The man that folks have been expecting to do the job has already proved he can't do it. Sitting around and waiting for the traditional politicians to do the job is like waiting for Frankenstein to change a baby's diaper. The monster is already loose in the land and the people have to take things in their own hands. We have to lock the monster up in the house and take care of business.

That's what things like the Black Caucus is all about. Black folks getting together and talking about the problems confronting America, problems that have been confronting us for a long time. But we're talking about all the problems, going back to the beginning. The Indian locked up on the reservation. As long as the Indian is up on the reservation, none of us are free. We've got to be talking about the problems of all oppressed people, not just some of the oppressed. Anytime I come and say I'm going to help you, and you notice I still haven't taken care of my own kids, you've got to be suspicious.

What began as a civil-rights movement has now been kicked up to the higher level of a *human*-rights movement. I learned that thanks to some beautiful people in Alabama and elsewhere in the South. We are all born into this world either male or female. When that happens, Nature has done her work. Created you either male or female and given you the creative capacity to reproduce and replenish the earth.

Moving up to a higher level is up to the individual. It happened to me when some wonderful people gave me some invitations to come down South and march and demonstrate for civil rights and human dignity. I was happy being a boy, standing on the corner, talking cool and being slick. Then the invitation came, and I didn't have anything to do with it. I got involved. A good feeling began running through me and I realized the real values in life. And I moved up to the next level. I had always been a male, but when I got involved in the struggle for human dignity, I became a man.

And that's what getting it together is all about. Moving up to that next level, beyond being a male or a female, and reaching the full stature of manhood and womanhood. Once you become a man or become a woman, you will work from that day on to make this world a better place for *all* of your fellow human beings and unborn babies who will inherit the world you have worked to create.

Chapter 6

COALITIONS—THE POLITICS OF THE FUTURE

by Shirley Chisholm

WORKING TOGETHER

The struggle which Black Americans encounter in our attempts to gain eonomic and political power in the United States must be fought on many different fronts. As a member of Congress, my fighting is done in the legislative arena. The Urban League fights in the business community and the National Association for the Advancement of Colored People fights in the courts. The Committee for a Unified Newark limits its scope to one urban area, whereas the Students' Organization for Black Unity reaches out for young Blacks on college campuses throughout the country.

Black student unions on various college campuses limit their action to the immediate community around the campus. The National Welfare Rights Organization is a nationwide phenomenon.

All of these groups, committees and caucuses have the same basic goals in mind: the liberation of Black people from oppression in the United States; the recognition of a unique Black culture; the creation of a climate in which Blacks will develop into productive adults with wholesome identities based on pride for themselves and for their race; economic and job security; and political power and influence in order to gain control of their own destinies.

These are minimal goals whose realization is long overdue. There are, however, different perceptions about how best to go about accomplishing these goals. That is why Blacks are working in diverse groups and on different levels toward more or less the same outcome. What the different approaches toward the same goal also display are the strong diversity of thought within the Black community and the intense political awareness which we have acquired. Hence, there is no reason to worry, as some persons do, because there is no one absolute approach to be taken.

Each of us is conditioned for dealing with problems in ways that reflect our individual personalities. What we must not do is to confuse the methods with the ends, which, fortunately, we have not done to date. Although I function in establishment politics, I seek to infuse new ideas into our antiquated procedures by holding onto the independent politics I learned in Brooklyn. Which is to say that my election to Congress was not supported by the clubhouse politicians who have been the backbone of the Democratic machine in Brooklyn. My campaign centered around the discussion of issues pertinent to the redevelopment of slum areas and innovations in education, an area of particular concern to me since I was an educator for sixteen years before entering politics. My election was not the result of support from any machine or any other reactionary political device. As a result, I am able to perform my duties with a great deal more independence than that which politicians usually possess.

Politics today—and particularly politics in Black communities—is beginning to open up to more issue-oriented candidates, thus affording an opportunity for more potential candidates who want to deal with the problems which this country faces. In the past, it has been an occupation for persons who want to hold to the *status quo*. Even so, the political arena lacks a great deal in so far as making basic changes in the system is concerned. Not yet has establishment politics addressed itself to such radical—and necessary—issues as the redistribution of wealth in America and proportional representation in government for all easily identifiable groups.

THE POLITICAL TASK

Surely, the impression should not be given that politics is where all the action is as far as advancing the cause of equality or equity for Blacks in the United States is concerned. Politics is not necessarily a panacea for the lack of self-respect and dignity which some of our people do not yet have as a result of having been brainwashed into believing that Black is somehow innately inferior to white. Politics is, in itself, no cure for the failure of many Blacks not to appreciate the wholesome culture which is ours. It is, however, the area in which I feel that I can make a contribution in attaining justice for Black Americans, bearing in mind that the relevant Black politician possesses five important criteria:

1. He possesses a firm understanding of the needs of the people to whom he appeals for election in order to fight for their interests in the arena to which he aspires.

2. He has some confidence—not always great—that the political arena for which he aspires can be made responsive to the needs of minorities, the poor and the other oppressed groups.

3. He believes that even though the arena which he seeks to enter is likely to be dominated by white males, replete with their narrow cultural values, he will still be able to maneuver in such a way that he can deliver basic services to the Black community and continue to assert his own Black identity in the process.

4. He must be realistic in assessing what he is likely to accomplish on his own. Indeed, because of the paucity of Blacks involved, and given the nature of politics— with its great emphasis on compromise and trading favors ("I'll support your bill on air pollution if you support my bill on comprehensive child-care facilities") —one must cultivate friends from groups other than Black ones before he can accomplish anything which is beneficial to the Black community.

5. He must possess the power of persuasion, which is tantamount to saying that he must be able to assert

points logically and coherently in order to impress upon his colleagues the rectitude of his position.

All these criteria are important ingredients in the makeup of the Black political being if he is to: (a) represent the pronounced interests of the Black community and (b) be a successful maneuverer in the political arena. It is no easy job to reconcile these two duties in view of the impatience of the Black community in acquiring its fair or equitable share of economic and political power in the United States and in view of the reluctance shown by whites in accommodating the just demands of the Black community.

GRASSROOTS NEEDS

As a Black politician, I feel that my most important task is to work to create a climate within the American society where Blacks, native Americans (Indians), Chicanos, Puerto Ricans, women and the poor can have strong voices within the decision-making process. Too long have these groups and their interests been ignored, while the interests of big business, industry and the very wealthy have been well taken care of by elected officials on all levels of government.

There is strong sentiment in my Congressional district in Brooklyn which suggests that government—on all levels—is unresponsive to the needs of the people, whether it is a matter of the city providing sanitation services or the state appropriating sufficient funds for education and welfare or the national government making an unequivocal commitment to end discrimination and injustices against minorities, the poor and women. In general, government in America does not respond to the needs of those Americans who fall into one of the categories—Black, Puerto Rican, Mexican-American, native Americans (Indians), women and the poor— where the full political potential of that category has not been felt. Nor will the political process be made more responsive until minorities, the poor and women organize effective campaigns to elect officials on all levels of government who are responsive to their interests.

Such groups as the Congressional Black Caucus and the National Women's Caucus have been formed in attempts to present unified fronts on issues which concern them. What these forces seek to do is to seize influence in the process by which decisions are made in the United States and, in so doing, guarantee that the interests of the constituencies which these forces represent will be taken into consideration by policy-makers.

Having served in the United States House of Representatives for two terms and in the New York State Assembly for four years prior to my service in Congress, I am well aware of the impact which interest groups may have on legislators and upon the executive as well. All politicians who think it is important to stay abreast of their constituents' thinking are likely to be impressed by groups which are organized on grassroots levels and who show that they can deliver or withhold support for the legislator. Grassroots organizations are effective weapons for countering the great and disproportionate influence of business and industry over the affairs of government. Whereas business and industry are quite generous in contributing substantial sums of money to the campaigns of their favorite legislators as a way of gathering influence with the legislator, grassroots organizations gain influence by being able to deliver votes to favored candidates at election periods.

A MORE REPRESENTATIVE GOVERNMENT

Yet I do not believe that we will have a truly effective Congress and system of government, too, until it is composed of more persons who are representative of the population in terms of race and sex. At the least, 50 percent of the members of the House should be women, given the fact that women compose more than half of the population of the United States. Proportional representation for Blacks would render forty-five Blacks in the House rather than the present thirteen. The House would not continue to be the conservative body that it is were these groups, as well as native Americans, Puerto Ricans and Mexican-Americans, represented in the House of Representatives in proportion to their population in the country as a whole.

Oppressed groups cannot depend upon anyone other than themselves to rectify the injustices in our society or to speak for them in Congress. Thus, it is essential that we rely upon our own political acumen in pursuing our claims and promoting our interests. Julian Bond asserts that "Appeals to justice and fair play are outmoded and useless when power, financial gain and prestige are at stake." That is exactly what oppressed groups are contending for at this time. Statistics show that no mere appeal to conscience or to reason will persuade those who hold the reins of power to relinquish any of the power which they have accumulated, even if some of it should be distributed to others.

Oppressed groups are constantly being informed that "remarkable" strides are being made toward bringing about a more equitable distribution of wealth and power in the United States. One is, however, not impressed with these strides if discrimination continues to retard his advancement. Recent statistics show that during the decade from 1960–1969, the number of Americans —of all colors—living in poverty reached 25.5 million, or one-eighth of the entire population. Poverty here is defined as an income below $3,968 for a nonfarm family of four. This is a considerably more restricting assessment of subsistence living than the Department of Labor's lower-level living standard for a family of four in New York, which is $7,183. Moreover, there are figures which show the continued economic disparity between Blacks and whites. While the medium income for whites is $9,974, the median income for Blacks is $6,191. A white with an eighth-grade education earned $7,018, which is more than the $6,192 earned by a Black with a high-school diploma. Unemployment for whites in 1970 was 4.5 percent, while unemployment for Blacks in the same year was 8.2 percent. The high-school dropout rate for whites was 6.7 percent, while the rate was 15.9 percent for Blacks.

The validity of these figures, coupled with an understanding of the long hard fight which made these meager "gains" possible, suggests to the members of the Congressional Black Caucus that we cannot let up in calling attention to the needs of Black Americans and other minority groups, in addition to proposing legislation which will speed the process of closing the gap between white and nonwhite economic status in the United States. Thus, the Caucus has played a leading role in opposing welfare "reform" that lacks adequate financial benefits to recipients; in supporting the establishment of day-care centers across the country so that mothers with pre-school children who want to work can have their children taken care of while working; in opposing the military adventures of foreign policy-makers, particularly in view of the $125 billion-plus Vietnam adventure; in opposing the Lockheed bail-out and the SST; and in seeking to emphasize the need to take care of social problems at home before engaging in efforts to force others abroad to accept the American way of life.

MUTUAL SELF-INTEREST

The Caucus—like Black America in general—is not a powerful group on its own; but it is developing coalitions with other minorities and progressive-minded whites. Blacks need not compromise what Julian Bond calls "racial self-interest." Rather, entrance into coalitions should be prompted out of the belief that on many issues, the concern of groups other than Black ones is just as great as our own. For instance, the Caucus has steadfastly opposed the war in Indochina because of its cost and illegality. We have joined with anti-war Congressmen and peace groups to express our opposition to American involvement. We have united our efforts with women's groups to propose that more and better day-care facilities be made available so that working mothers, regardless of race and economic status, will not be restricted in performing their jobs because of the absence of provisions for the care of their children. We have supported the efforts of rank-and-file Democrats to appropriate funds for the creation of public-service jobs to ease the rising tide of unemployment. And we have supported welfare recipients in attempting to make provisions for adequate public-assistance benefits for all of our nation's poor.

Moreover, because I am both Black and a woman, I have taken a great deal of interest in the women's movement. Particularly, the economic issues raised by women's groups need thoughtful attention. The infrequency of women advancing beyond positions of clerical work suggests unequal employment practices. Opportunities for advancement to top positions in most fields are reserved for white males, while women and minority groups must settle for the less prestigious and lesser-paying positions. Figures on the employment of women illustrate that they, too, suffer from discrimination and injustice at the hands of white males. Although women make up over 51 percent of the population in the country, only 37 percent of the professional and technical positions in the American society are held by women. Eighty-two percent of employed women are in clerical, sales, factory, farm and service occupations. Six percent are medical and health workers, college teachers or other professional and technical workers. Only 5 percent are managers, officials or proprietors. Reasons submitted for the discrepancy between the number of women in top positions and the percentage of their population in the country amount to little more than myths which suggest that women are too fragile and too emotional to advance to the higher echelons in the job market. No statistics are offered to support such suggestions; thereby, one is left to doubt the legitimacy of the contention.

Discrimination against females is doubly burdensome to Black women, who are left at the very bottom of the job market and its attending pay scale. With 29 percent of Black households headed by a female, it is dubious that the economic ascension of Blacks can transpire without a complementary economic ascension to the status of American women. For this reason, I am unable to make a clear-cut separation between the struggles of Blacks and the struggles of women against discrimination within the American society.

Indeed, discrimination remains the great evil in our society, for it is the shield behind which white males harbor their racism and sexism and guard their disproportionate share of wealth and power in the country. Moreover, this discrimination is accompanied by attempts to superimpose their WASP-oriented values on other groups who are no longer willing to tolerate such imposition. Women will no longer settle for secretarial positions when they are qualified for executive roles. Puerto Ricans and Mexican-Americans will not refrain from speaking Spanish simply because it is not the official language of the country. Blacks will not forsake their racial identity just to make an attempt to fit into an alien culture. In summary, no oppressed group is any longer willing to assume the role which the dominating group would have it assume.

SERVING HUMAN NEEDS

It is the failure of American society to open its door to cultural plurality which has spawned the antagonism which exists between the "establishment" and various oppressed groups. The goal of these groups is the expression of their values, whether or not these values reflect the prevailing notions of the WASP-oriented establishment, without forfeiting their rights to equitable wealth, political power, justice and liberty in the society as a whole. These goals are mine as well—for which reason I align myself with enlightened groups that also believe in equal rights, self-determination and the freedom to express one's identity in whatever way one chooses that is compatible with peaceful coexistence between individuals and groups.

I am, however, ever mindful that my first priority is the liberation of Blacks from second-class status in America. It should be obvious to anyone who has visited certain parts of my district in Brooklyn that the very survival of human beings is at stake. An employment rate of 41 percent in some parts of Bedford-Stuyvesant and Brownsville, lead poisoning, rat bites, drug addiction, inferior schools and incessant crime leave many persons—most unfortunately many young children are among them—hopeless and without motivation. It is such dismal problems as these which require my most immediate attention. But the struggle still continues on a larger scene, involving those who live in Appalachia, in Southwestern barrios and on Indian reservations. It is precisely the fact that the struggle needs all the forces it can assemble which makes coalition desirable at this point.

Chapter 7

PORTUGAL INVADES GUINEA: THE FAILURE OF U.S. POLICY TOWARD AFRICA

by John Conyers, Jr.

On December 8, 1970, the United States abstained from voting on the United Nations Security Council resolution which condemned Portugal's November 22 invasion of the Republic of Guinea. The resolution declared Portuguese colonialism a serious threat to the peace and security of independent African states, demanded that Portugal pay reparations to Guinea, urged an embargo on all military assistance to Portugal and warned Portugal that in the event of further armed attacks against independent African states, the Security Council would immediately consider appropriate sanctions. The resolution passed unanimously, with the U. S., France, Britain and Spain abstaining.

SHIELD OF AGGRESSION

This episode is the most dramatic example of the United States' failure to alter her policy toward Portugal and its colonial empire of Angola, Mozambique and Guinea-Bissau. The U. S. has continued to supplement the dangerous international anachronism to which Portugal clings with our own backward and misguided approach. This essay will show our foreign policy toward Portugal has failed and what must be done to fulfill the promise of the American ideal of self-determination for all peoples.

Although Portugal denied involvement in the November invasion of Guinea, the case against her was and is hardly controversial. The five-member UN Special Mission charged with responsibility for investigating and reporting the situation unanimously concluded that on the night of November 21-22, 1970, the Republic of Guinea was invaded from the sea by a force consisting of "units of the Portuguese armed forces, mainly African troops from Guinea-Bissau under the command of regular white Portuguese officers, as well as a contingent composed of dissident Guineans trained and armed on the territory of Guinea-Bissau."

In addition to the evidence presented by the UN Special Mission, United States intelligence sources are reported to have independently confirmed Portugal's role in the invasion. Just prior to this vote on the Security Council resolution, Ambassador Yost, U.S. representative to the United Nations, stated that the United States did not question to Special Mission's judgment concerning responsibility for the attack. The U. S. abstained on the vote, however, due to the reluctance of our government to authorize consideration of United Nations sanctions against Portugal. The U. S. took particular exception to the provision in the resolution which "solemnly warns the Government of Portugal that in the event of any repetition of armed attacks against independent African states, the Security Council shall immediately consider appropriate effective steps or measures in accordance with the relevant provisions of the United Nations Charter." The original draft of this provision stated that the Security Council would respond to a repetition of Portuguese attacks by invoking Chapter VII of the United Nations Charter. Chapter VII provides that when the Security Council has determined the existence of any threat to the peace, breach of the peace or act of aggression, it may decide to take measures, including the use of armed force, to maintain or restore international peace and security. When the United States threatened to veto the original draft resolution, the Afro-Asian sponsors deleted the direct reference to Chapter VII. Still unsatisfied, apparently because the threat of UN sanctions against Portugal remained, the United States abstained on the vote.

To understand the American objection to the possibility of invoking United Nations sanctions against Portugal, the U.S. abstention must be reviewed in relation to the position the United States has maintained toward Portuguese military activities in Africa ever since the outbreak of rebellions in the Portuguese territories in the early 1960's. American officials have always treated the Portuguese armed repression of the liberation movements as a potential rather than a current threat to international peace, indeed, often not wanting to consider it at all. On this basis, the United States has consistently opposed all United Nations resolutions which would authorize sanctions to force Portugal to cease her colonial wars and take steps toward granting independence to the more than 13 million people in her territories. At the same time that the American government verbally supports the principle that the peoples of these territories have a "legitimate right to self-determination" little or nothing is done to persuade the Portuguese to accept it in practice. Portugal officially denies that the United Nations even has the right to consider the situation in her African colonies because she defines these lands as an integral part of Portugal and therefore not subject to international law. For over a decade Portugal has ignored UN resolutions demanding that she accept her international responsibilities under the UN Charter to prepare her colonies for independence and instead has engaged in brutal repression of the independence movements which have been fighting for their people's right of self-government. In pursuing these colonial wars, Portugal has perpetrated numerous attacks on independent African states. Guinea's report of the November 22, 1970, invasion was the fourth official accusation of Portuguese attacks brought before the Security Council by independent African states during the space of a single year. Even so, the United States has always insisted that verbal persuasion is the only appropriate means for dealing with Portugal and has refused to support any of the economic or other sanctions which have been proposed in various United Nations resolutions.

It is in this context that we must interpret Ambassador Yost's official explanation of the U.S. abstention:

> In the view of the United States, the draft resolution does not constitute a finding that a Chapter VII situation exists, nor could it commit the Council to taking action under Chapter VII in any future situation. Nevertheless, the draft resolution does seem to us to go much too far in this direction and to create presumptions about our future actions, in a very broad range of situations, which are not warranted at this time.

In other words, the United States does not consider Portugal's armed invasion of an independent African state a grave enough situation to warrant even the consideration of sanctions by the United Nations Security Council. This refusal to accept reality not only carries with it implicit support for Portuguese actions but releases that country from any fear of effective condemnation. On December 19, 1970, eleven days after the Security Council vote, Guinea's President, Mr. Sekou Toure, cabled United Nations Secretary General U Thant to report that Portuguese troops were again massing on Guinea's borders, apparently preparing to launch an attack on Guinean airfields and population centers. Previously many Western diplomats had felt that the United Nations Special Mission's report confirming Portugal's responsibility for the November 22 invasion and the resulting Security Council resolution would deter further Portuguese attacks on Guinea, at least for the near future.

SERVING HUMAN NEEDS

It appears, however, that Portugal interprets the refusal of the United States, Britain and France to support the United Nations resolution as a signal that she can continue aggression in Africa without fear of Western-backed sanctions. This development gives added urgency to the need of a re-evaluation of the American abstention and of U.S. policy toward Portugal in general.

CIRCUITOUS JUSTIFICATION

Another consequence of this lethargic policy is the increasing resentment on the part of many Africans toward the Western powers who refused to support the Afro-Asian-sponsored resolution. Immediately after the December 8, 1970, vote in the Security Council, Guinea's representative said:

> The debate which has just taken place goes far beyond my own little country. These events are a final warning to the Security Council that it must safeguard international peace and security. Must the African countries consider that their defense and security will have to depend on the sympathy and esteem they enjoy from those who unconditionally support Portugal?
>
> Portugal has committed an act of open and flagrant armed aggression against the sovereignty and integrity of a Member State. The Charter of the United Nations —our Charter—in its Chapter VII provides for the appropriate sanctions to be taken in such a case; but since it is an African State, certain members of the Council have felt that to invoke Chapter VII . . . would

go beyond what decisions or measures could or should be taken when an African State falls victim to an aggression.

The Security Council resolution, in urging "all States to refrain from providing the government of Portugal with any military and material assistance enabling it to continue its repressive actions against the peoples of the territories under its domination and against independent African States," attempted to deal directly with Portugal's military ability to launch these armed attacks against sovereign African states.

The United States objected to the clear implication in this provision of the Security Council resolution that the NATO allies should terminate the military aid and arms sales they make to Portugal as a NATO partner. Because the U. S. is not willing to sever its NATO ties with Portugal, American officials make the argument that in 1961 the Kennedy Administration imposed an embargo on shipments of American arms to Portugal for use in Africa. Since that time Portugal has given assurances that new American equipment is used only in the NATO area. Therefore, the U. S., in its own view, is not contributing to Portugal's military activities in Africa. During the debate on the Security Council resolution, Ambassador Yost asserted that the United States' ban on arms to Portugal for use in Africa "fully meets the objectives" of the provision urging an embargo on military aid to Portugal, and that "any effort to broaden the scope of the Council's recommendations concerning assistance to Portugal would be unjustified . . . and not in the interests of the people of the African territories under Portuguese control."

SERVING HUMAN NEEDS

The U. S. understood full well that the Afro-Asian sponsors of the Security Council resolution intended to demand the termination of NATO aid to Portugal. In the four days of debate prior to the adoption of the resolution, the African delegates repeatedly charged that Western military aid, supposedly intended for NATO defense purposes, plays a major role in Portugal's military activities in Africa. On December 7, the representative from Uganda stated:

> My delegation and several other delegations have repeatedly stated in this Council and in the various Committees of the General Assembly that Portugal alone could not effectively subdue the liberation movements in Guinea-Bissau, Angola and Mozambique. It is the support that the NATO Powers give Portugal that makes that poor country proud and impervious to reason. It is because of NATO support that Portugal undertook an invasion of the Republic of Guinea. It is because of NATO support that Portugal ignores all the resolutions that have been adopted by this Council and the General Assembly.

The Republic of Zambia shares borders with the Portuguese territories of Angola and Mozambique and has suffered numerous armed attacks on its territory by Portuguese military forces. During the debate on the Security Council resolution, Zambia's representative charged:

> Portugal's crimes against independent Africa are also NATO's crimes against Africa. There are no two ways about that. It is with NATO arms and material assistance that an impoverished Portugal is waging

its colonial wars and committing acts of aggression against independent African States.

America's circuitous justification for continuing military aid to Portugal while at the same time claiming not to be contributing to the tremendous military force Portugal employs in Africa was summarily dismissed in the following comments of the representative of the Sudan:

> The evidence is too overwhelming to be hidden behind a haze of mystifying declarations and window-dressing statements that we hear time and again from NATO powers. Our brothers in Africa are being killed, maimed and dragged into bloody servitude by British Lockheeds, American B-26 bombers, German Fouga magister jets, French frigates and Panhard armored cars. And while we are meeting here to consider Portuguese aggression against an African country, three 1,400-ton warships destined for Portuguese colonies are being built at the West German shipyards of Blohm and Voss, possibly to transport more mercenaries and armies of invasion into other African harbors. Yesterday it was the Congo, Tanzania, Zambia and Senegal. Today it is Guinea. The whole of Africa is asking, whose turn tomorrow?

The United States justifies its military aid to Portugal by citing Portuguese assurances that American aid is used only in the NATO area—i.e., Europe. We assume, of course, that Europe is not Africa. Portugal, however, makes no such logical distinction. She regards the mission of her armed forces as the defense of her national territory, which includes, by her own definition, the so-called "overseas provinces" of Angola, Mozambique and

Guinea-Bissau. Other NATO allies also achieve a like level of complicity with their own definitional disagreements. In 1966, Germany supplied Portugal with forty Fiat G-21 fighter planes and stated that "the planes are to be used exclusively in Portugal for defense purposes within the framework of the North Atlantic Pact." A spokesman for the Portuguese Foreign Ministry gave this interpretation:

> The transaction was agreed within the spirit of the North Atlantic Pact. It was agreed that the planes would be used only for defensive purposes within Portuguese territory. Portuguese territory extends to Africa —Angola, Mozambique and Portuguese Guinea.

MUTUALLY SUPPORTIVE GOALS

The U.S. argument for continued aid to Portugal depends on the assumption that Portugal's military role in Europe is quite separate from its role in Africa. This is simply untrue. Since the beginning of the colonial rebellions in the early 1960's, Portugal has stationed two-thirds to three-quarters of her armed forces in the African territories, with the regular units of the Portuguese army generally serving two years in Africa before being rotated back to Europe. According to the latest statistics compiled by the Institute of Strategic Studies in London, at least 125,000 of Portugal's 185,000-man armed forces are presently in Africa. For the past several years Portugal has been spending at least 40 to 50 percent of her annual budget on the defense of her overseas possessions. A major function of Portugal's air force and navy is troop transport between Europe and Africa. With the exception of one NATO-assigned, anti-submarine reconnaissance squadron, the entire Portuguese air force is in her colonies. Similarly, the navy —composed of U.S.-, French- and German-built destroyers, patrol boats and minesweepers—is more useful for anti-rebel missions along the coast of Africa than for any NATO maneuver in Europe.

One of the most telling American contributions to the Portuguese African effort is the training its officers receive under our Military Assistance Program, most of which takes place in the U. S. In 1969, 133 Portuguese received training under this program; in fiscal 1970, thirty members of their military were so trained, and while it has been reported that our State Department has a general policy of not allowing Portuguese counter-insurgency training in the U. S., since the early 1960's all military courses have some counter-insurgency classes. Therefore, all Portuguese trained in the U. S. gain some direct experience in the type of warfare being employed by their country in her colonies. These facts belie the U.S. assertion that it is not contributing to Portugal's armed aggression in Africa.

The Western Powers' attempt to exempt NATO military contributions to Portugal from the Security Council's proposed embargo on all military aid to Portugal was censured by virtually every independent African state with the understandable exception of Rhodesia and South Africa. On December 11, 1970, the Ministerial Council of the forty-one-member Organization of African Unity unanimously passed a resolution directly condemning the "NATO powers which allow, through their complicity and assistance, various attacks by Portugal against several African territories and states." The OAU resolution called upon the NATO powers to withdraw all assistance to Portugal.

Why does the United States refuse to take this minimal step to curb Portuguese armed aggression in Africa? Why does it continue to base its military relations with Portugal on vague "assurances" by that totalitarian colonial regime that our arms are not used in her African territories, and officially disregard African assertions to the contrary? The rationale for this posture becomes clearer when we consider the role the United States military plays in shaping American policy toward Portugal.

How could the Department of Defense support the use of sanctions against an invasion whose objective was in part to free Portuguese prisoners, when units of the United States armed forces on the night of November 20-21, 1970, the very night before the Portuguese invasion of Guinea, raided the North Vietnamese prison at Sontay in an abortive attempt to free American prisoners? The Washington *Post* reported that President Nixon told a soldier at the White House Thanksgiving dinner that "the possibility of more raids should not be overlooked." Little wonder that the United States refuses to support the threat of United Nations sanctions against Portugal for engaging in an operation so similar in intent to its own.

Another objective of Portugal's invasion of Guinea cited by the UN Special Mission was "to strike at the leadership and headquarters of the PAIGC and thus weaken the liberation movement." President Nixon, in announcing the United States' invasion of Cambodia on April 30, 1970, said: "Tonight American and South Vietnamese units will attack the headquarters for the entire Communist military operations in South Vietnam." The President asserted that the American goal was not to occupy territory in the neutral state of Cambodia, but to drive out enemy forces and destroy their sanctuaries. The parallel between the objectives and actions of the Americans in Cambodia and the Portuguese in Guinea is clear. The United States invaded the neutral country of Cambodia; the Portuguese invaded the sovereign state of Guinea. How can the one condemn the other without at the same time condemning itself?

U.S. MILITARISM AND RACISM

Militarism and racism have been prime ingredients in the development of American policy toward Portugal. In spite of Portugal's brutal repression of her subject people's demands for independence, and in spite of her many armed attacks on independent African states, the United States has continued to supply this unyielding colonial power with military and economic aid, $7.5 million in 1969. Since 1963 we have voted no or abstained on all United Nations resolutions condemning Portugal's colonial policy or her attacks on African states. The Defense Department continues to inculcate American foreign policy with the cold-war emphasis on military strength and so-called "stability or maintenance of the *status quo* in the Third World." The State Department's assertion in various official documents that "the United States recognizes the contribution made in Africa by Portugal, and believes it is important that Portugal continue to contribute to the stability and progress in that Continent" speaks to the racist character of our policy, when considered against the reality of Portugal's decade-long colonial wars in all her African territories.

The military argument for supporting Portugal is becoming less and less tenable. The original basis for her admission to NATO was Portugal's control of several islands in the Atlantic, principally the Azores. But by all accounts, the Azores' strategic value has declined steadily since the beginning of the 1960's when 80 percent of U.S. military transports en route to Europe refueled there. With the advent of longer-range aircraft a stopping point in the Atlantic is no longer essential and the role of our Azores bases has shifted primarily to the maintenance of a naval reconnaissance and rescue operation. Although now unnecessary for its original purpose, the Pentagon can always find a new use, however marginal, for old military bases. But if from fear of losing a strategic position in the Azores the United States was ever justified in refraining from taking truly persuasive action against Portugal's colonial policies, it clearly is not the case presently. The Azores are of minimal value at best and certainly cannot equal the significance of the implicit support we are giving to Portugal's transgressions against humanity in Africa.

With regard to NATO, Portugal appears to be more interested in what can be obtained from membership in this pact than in making a contribution to European security. At present Portugal earmarks only one division of its armed forces for NATO duty in time of war. This division was only at 50 percent strength in 1969 and represented only about 10 percent of total Portuguese troops. The fact that the U.S. State Department recognizes the low priority Portugal places on her NATO responsibilities was plainly indicated in a November 13, 1970, letter to Senator Clifford Case. The letter stated, "Without our MAP [Military Assistance Program], Portugal's NATO proficiency would likely suffer, while there would be virtually no effect on its capability in Africa." Obviously, Portugal is no longer an important NATO ally, if it ever was.

The failure of the U. S. to respond meaningfully to the Portuguese invasion of Guinea can be seen as part of a larger indictment of American foreign policy in failing to keep pace with the changing international considerations of the 1970's. Ignored is the fundamental recognition that political independence and meaningful social and economic development are crucial factors in maintaining political stability and peaceful development. The U. S. has continued to base its foreign policy on cold-war assumptions that European interests, even those of a colonial regime seeking desperately to hold onto its African empire with blatantly illegal armed aggression, always take priority over purely African interests. It is difficult to escape the conclusion that the United States, with its domestically racist attitudes, cannot help but project that same sentiment in terms of its relations with African nations. This racist approach has alienated forty-one independent African states by seeking to maintain the allegiance of an insignificant fascist regime. The U. S. has obstructed the attempt of the Third World to seek justice and protection against external aggression by employing the machinery of the United Nations and has thereby weakened that world body as a result.

Chapter 8

NEWARK AND WE

by Kenneth A. Gibson

OUR PLIGHT

If one question comes to mind after one and a half years as Mayor of Newark, that one question is: Does the United States of America really give a damn?

This question is asked with honesty. The honest answer to this question will determine the nature of the future. It will help determine how civilized the United States of America is capable of becoming. With urban deterioration accelerating at its present rate, the answer to this question must be given by powerful men in many high places. The absolute weight of that answer will press fully on their shoulders. There will be no Black Simon to help carry that cross.

On one hand, I recognize my election as Mayor of

Newark, New Jersey, as relatively conventional in a political sense—another example of how the "melting pot" never really melted. I am elected to represent all of the people of the city of Newark. This responsibility I recognize and do my best to fulfill. Of course, there are people whose political motives will not allow them to understand or believe this.

On the other hand, I recognize my election as Mayor of the city of Newark as an extension of the revolt of slaves aboard a slave ship. Because we first sailed the sea of "civilization" as slaves, no self-respecting Black can refuse to recognize himself as a part of this total history. No Black elected official who chooses to remain responsive to the total needs of an entire nation can allow that history of struggle to blind him to the possibilities of the future.

When we begin to discuss this future, we are faced with the proposition of probability and possibility versus improbability and impossibility. It is possible that every individual urban problem facing the United States could be reduced to a manageable level. It is impossible to see how this can be done under existing conditions, given present attitudes and lack of commitment. It is probable that a group of men who can see these possibilities will come to growth out of the current urban crisis. In the least, it is improbable that these men will gain the power to move these possibilities into realities. The nation itself will have to reevaluate its moral concepts in order to bring about such profound change.

As you read this essay, it is highly probable that before you finish it a child will die at birth. Newark has the highest rate of infant mortality in this nation. It is improbable that this condition will change in the foreseeable future. The diabolical ugliness of this truth is found in the fact that this is a condition which has existed in Newark, without significant change, since the 1930's. Our women can go from the time of conception to the very day the child is born without one hour of pre-natal medical care. Could this happen in a truly civilized land? There are people who seek answers to this disgraceful condition. We must question why the problem exists in the first place. We must question the civility of the source of the problem. It does not start with an ill-cared-for mother. It is only when we can find our way through this labyrinth of social backwardness that we will actually be prepared to develop adequate solutions.

In the United States, the nation as a whole has allowed itself the luxury of equating technology to civilization. This has been a face-saving device. Further, to support this notion, this nation has been able to convince the citizenry that there is a relationship between the lack of technology and being uncivilized. This prejudice has allowed us to glory in our own technological self-righteousness. In the cities of America, we can see that there is not necessarily a relationship between technology and civilization.

While technology heads directly for a precise landing place on the moon, social advancement, which is reflective of the nation's level of civilization, meanders pointlessly throughout the urban areas of our country. Civilization barely reaches the edge of the technological hard-core ghettos. "Civilization" stands at the edge and laughs in the face of the people.

I was born in Alabama and raised in Newark. These

problems are nothing new to me. The glaring reality that these problems have trailed Black people throughout the centuries is extremely disturbing to me. Arm in arm with other Blacks and concerned people, we have had political, civil-rights and social organizations which have fought to have this city rebuilt. In an effort to refine living in Newark, we struggled to correct some of the malpractices of government. Unfortunately, at the very same time we were making the struggle, the city was being torn down from around us. The city was deaf to the voices of humanity which rose out of its own squalor.

In the absence of civilized progress, deterioration is bound to rule. There was nothing sudden or abrupt about the retrogression of Newark. There were many who saw the direction in which the city was moving and tried to alter that direction. Unfortunately, there were those in government and other high places who, for their own reasons and interests, paid no heed to our efforts. Callously, they decided to let the city go to hell!

A SOCIALLY RESPONSIBLE SYSTEM

Having come out of a tradition of hand-me-downs and leftovers, many people in the Black community have urged us to refuse to accept these secondhand cities. This advice I refused to accept. I became Mayor of Newark knowing fully the vastness of Newark's problems. This responsibility does not frighten me, but there are frightful obstacles in the way of any man who accepts this responsibility. In fairness, not all of these obstacles have been placed in the road to impede the march to civilization. Quite often, they occurred much like the senseless pattern of street development in many cities. These obstructions occurred because no one planned for a more sensible pattern.

In other cases, elected, public and business officials have devised schemes, meeting until the wee hours of the morning planning plots to spring bear traps on the legs of people climbing to a higher socio-economic plateau. The final goal of these schemes is to keep the powerless powerless. Moreover, these men of power use this powerlessness as a means of undercutting the progress of people. There are still men meeting for these anti-human purposes, even though this nation heads toward the brink of social disaster. They will probably still be meeting when time knocks on their door to announce their end. Yes, many people will "go to their graves to make sure that they are dead."

I make the assumption that competitive, profitable, private enterprise can exist side by side with a socially responsible system. In fact, an elevated social system is private enterprise's best security for the future. We have models of this possibility in countries like Denmark, Norway and Sweden. We of the urban centers must ask the creators of obstacles, the worshipers of power:

Why shouldn't our children eat properly?

Why should children die at birth?

Why should a little boy not be afforded an educational system in which he can learn to read?

Or why shouldn't the nation consider the privilege of proper recreation one that all human beings should have?

SERVING HUMAN NEEDS

Why can't the nation recognize that once it allows anyone in its midst to drop below a certain quality of life, their very lowly existence, in the world's richest land, stands as a highly negative reflection on and threat to the civilization level of that land?

After taking a long overview of the problems which exist in the United States—the solutions to which are impeded by unbridled racism, ethnocentric thinking, egocentric self-seekers and the whole myriad of problems honest men could meet in finding satisfactory answers—we decided on a very practical course for the city of Newark. We would be pragmatic, without ever compromising our commitment to elevating the level of civilization. Our administration would use its time and effort attempting to give human beings the kind of daily service their needs demand. Of course, we recognized that this was not a total solution, by any means. If more were to be added, then we could expect to do much more.

If we decided, for an example, to keep the parks clean, one morning we would have to wake some desperate soul to sweep around him. Clean parks will not solve homelessness. Certainly the urban problems go beyond sweeping streets and picking up garbage. They are more complicated than knocking down dilapidated houses and improving medical care. The problems even go beyond providing children with an adequate education. The fact that we might improve snow clearance will mean very little to a mother who has to send her child out in the winter with canvas gym shoes on his feet.

Yet, if we improved services and got people to understand that this was their right as civilized human beings, they could become more conscious of their right to shape their lives. Better services was just a point at which to start. This was a point where visible accomplishments could be made which would improve the lives of the people. It would be a way of saying to nearly 400,000 people that the government recognizes your rights as people—people who deserve a certain level of civilized living. Certainly, no one could oppose such a meager meal for so many hungry people.

Our administration has decided to move forward to accomplish the goal of improved services, without wearing heavily the cross of powerlessness upon our shoulders. We will not curse the darkness. If we do not have the power to accomplish these basic changes to better human existence, it is not our powerlessness which is at fault. It is the misuse of power and resources on the part of others which remains at fault. Those with power will have to answer for this. Tragically, they seem to be waiting until masses of people are deaf to their voices.

THE NATIONAL ROLE

Structurally, we cannot provide improved services without the help of the national government. We hoped that this help would be forthcoming. The city needs help which is not complicated or incumbered. The Newark administration can certainly tell the federal government what we need and what should be done. Whether or not it will be done is beyond our control. The maze and mystery of government might cause national politics to be uncontrollable.

We could tell them that the present system of unemployment compensation should be modified. This could provide higher benefits, for a longer time, during inflation and high unemployment periods.

We could suggest that the federal government assume the full cost of all public-assistance programs, ensuring equal treatment throughout the country. We know that the present proposed minimum support level should be dramatically raised in an attempt to recognize, and deal with, the increased cost of providing a decent and adequate standard of living.

They should recognize that welfare reforms must be coupled with a national network of day-care centers, available to all of the people. Looking at the stretches of ruins in urban centers, it is obvious that Congress should declare housing disaster areas for various sections of the country. This must include the massive infusion of monies to acquire land, to develop housing and subsidize mortgages and to train men for employment.

Maybe all future federally funded housing should be sold to the people, not rented. The slumlord has completely relinquished his right to exist in the urban areas. Ruthless speculators in housing have absolutely forfeited their privilege of managing the earth in the urban areas. We need an end to absentee landlordism and to instill a sense of pride in ownership which is not totally lacking. It is impossible to be proud of some of the monstrosities called "public housing."

Irrespective of any opinions put forth by the federal administration, we know that wage-price controls are no substitute for revenue sharing. It is not a reason even to postpone the enactment of revenue sharing. An economic stimulant cannot save people existing outside the economy. Congress should enact immediately a revenue-sharing program. This should not replace existing categorical programs. The cities need new money, even if this money must be subject to the scrutiny of a committee of Congressman and Senators.

There is no reason why a country as wealthy as the United States should attempt to exist without a national health plan, the political pressures of the American Medical Association not withstanding.

If business itself cannot recognize a responsibility to human existence over and above *technolization* and profits, then we certainly hope that the Congress of the United States would give them tax incentives so that they would bring business back into the urban centers. Cities need the jobs which only business can create. Of course, big business can refuse to do this. However, no one can predict the outcome of people seeking political alternatives to this refusal. If the federal government could bring itself to move to this level of sophistication —to this level of humanity—the government certainly would have moved to new heights of civilization in the United States. The needs are so painfully obvious. The federal responses to those needs are so obviously lacking.

In the meantime, in Newark, we will continue to work with what we have. In some cases, what we have to work with will be new and bright and viable. We will be able to accomplish. In other cases, we will have to work with the old and immobile and practically hopeless. Certain elements of Newark's public and private sectors cannot accomplish that which our times demand.

On another level, what we can accomplish through our own resources will be limited by the position in which we find ourselves relative to state government. The city of Newark is a creature of the state of New Jersey. Hence, state laws supersede the city ordinances, rules and regulations. The building of a highway can take precedence over the building of city streets and push aside the building of needed housing. One gets the feeling that the needs of people were not even meant to dovetail with some of the priorities of government. If we just take the state's power in the matter of eminent domain, the state can condemn property in Newark to build a highway. The state of New Jersey has done just that. However, they did not build the highway. What they have done is to demolish housing, from which the city was receiving tax dollars, and to scatter the people who lived on these sites. Now nothing stands in these places but run-down lots. How civilized is a nation which evicts its people from their land and then allows that land to collect garbage? Through some means, we must find the way to bring the power of the state and the needs of the cities into a more equitable balance. This would change the state house in Trenton (New Jersey's capital city) from a partisan political power center into a center for solving the problems of people. This would make the state house relevant. Otherwise, the conflict between rural and suburban power and urban needs will be the source of endless turmoil.

The problems we grappled with in the first six months showed how low civilization had sunk in Newark. Ironically, I read in an editorial that now "the honeymoon was over." The newspaper was saying, "Well, we took it easy on you for the first six months, but now you are going to have to produce or suffer the wrath of your opponents." I couldn't help wondering what honeymoon they were talking about. From the first, we were confronted with a negative, malfunctioning, insensitive and corrupted government. The inherited administrative machinery was in a state of shambles. It was chaotic, archaic and almost totally unmanageable. If the first six months were to be looked upon as a honeymoon, we had certainly married an unfaithful bride.

So-called civilized public servants had stolen, mismanaged or wasted the money of the people of Newark. During that same "honeymoon" our administration had to deal with a fiscal crisis of unprecedented proportions. When we turned the key in the door, we anticipated a budget deficit of $65 million. As our honeymoon continued, we were hit by the longest and one of the most bitter school strikes this nation has ever seen. The dispute between the Board of Education and the Newark Teachers Union put many of our children out on the street. The racism in the air was more lethal than air pollution. In all of this, the lack of concern for the human needs of Newark's youngsters was appalling. It was unbelievable.

The administration was glad when the honeymoon was over.

The first year ended. It was time to take stock. I do not know what is so magic about twelve months, except that people have become accustomed to annual reports. The press wanted to know what we had done to remedy the problems it had taken scores of years to create. In keeping with the superman mentality which seeps into

SERVING HUMAN NEEDS

American thinking, they wanted to know whether or not I had tamed the wilderness. People, no matter where they found themselves on the social and economic ladder, were asking the same question. It was a question they were asking me, but the answer had to come from an entire society. In times of dire need, people will expect an elected administrator to be a miracle worker. When people need help, they will expect department heads of city government to become Houdinis who can unravel the entangled bureaucratic structure. Why not? They can't do it. This I can certainly understand.

WORKING WITH PEOPLE

When people cannot reach those who are responsible, they hold those responsible that they can reach.

City government is accessible. Newark city government is not as powerful as it is accessible. Since this is true, our administration's next major thrust will be to convince the citizens of Newark that they should work in combination with us, in order to reach our own established goals of improved civilization.

Perhaps the idea of government which wants to work with people, as opposed to dominating them, is too new or naïve-sounding to believe. Yet, this is the absolute goal of our administration. Perhaps an administration which expects the people who are appointed to work for the normal salary, without attempting to beg, borrow or steal an extra red penny, is moving against too much political tradition. Nonetheless, this is the expectation of our administration. This administration expects a full day's work from Civil Service employees who accept a full day's pay. We are certain that this is a totally new concept for some city employees. We also believe that the elected Mayor of city government should run the city. He should not waste the taxpayer's money by using his term as four years to run for re-election. As simple as all of these things sound, they are foreign to Newark politics. They are foreign to American politics in general. So again the question: Does the United States of America really give a damn?

This has been a cursory observation of our city government's relationships with federal, state and local bureaucracies. It has been oversimplified. Now what about me and my administration?

Speculation is an intrinsic part of politics. People are speculating about my possibilities for re-election if I ran tomorrow. Victory or defeat? I am told the responses have divided equally. There are those who would vote for me, others wouldn't. Since I am not running for re-election tomorrow and have not decided if I'll even run for re-election when the time rolls around, the question is academic at best. Of course, our administration had the choice of securing ourselves in the popularity polls by grinding out a certain amount of public-relations glitter, overblowing minor accomplishments and convincing the public we are doing things which we are not doing. Our administration has refused to do this. Our administration will be judged on the progress of people, not press clippings.

The Mayor of a city stands to be the most controversial man in town. Therefore, the more interesting question for me is whether or not any man who happened to have been elected Mayor of Newark in 1970 could be reelected in September, 1971, irrespective of his qualifications, energies, accomplishments and the number of problems he was burdened with at the time of his election. "Burdened" is a bad choice of a word. Someone had to stop the city from falling apart and attempt to save the people who lived in Newark. I have gone to public schools in Newark. I have seen the uncivilized way many people have been forced to live. I grew up in Newark and saw some of my friends lost in a system which did not care if they existed. So it was not a burden that I took upon myself when I asked the people to elect me Mayor, but a responsibility and a means of self-survival. There was little choice in May of 1970; the city had to be saved. It just might not be possible.

Let people be anxious to judge the administration after one and a half years. Let these same people be capable of analyzing what is possible within the framework of city government as it relates to state and federal government. This evaluation, based on real possibilities, I am perfectly willing to hear, consider and be influenced by. However, if people are going to approach the problems with the attitude "What have you done for me today?" or "What have you done for me recently?" their judgments are almost certain to be irrelevant.

We must determine whether the level of civilization in the United States is viable enough to halt the present deterioration. When our administration and the community start working together—and I believe this is highly possible—then we must come together based on our judgments of accomplishments which are possible in the United States. We must first analyze whether or not the city as an entity is a workable level of government at this point. Moreover, will the United States itself allow a growth pattern which will cure many of the social ills the cities suffer? And if not, is the situation such that we will have to develop programs for basic survival, programs which are designed to hold the community together until such time as we can move forward? If this is the case, we would have to become an active part of national politics to ensure urban survival.

In this case, when I speak of the community, I do not speak of the middle class, the lower class, the poor or the hungry. I speak of an entire community. Earlier I said that a civilized people cannot let any member of its community fall below a certain level without affecting its level of civilization. My appeal to the community is to be one. We must recognize that we are faced with the problem of the drug addict on the corner and the mugger who, for whatever reason, thinks he has the right or the need to take from someone else. We must help the mother who, because of poor health facilities or because of poor education, doesn't receive pre-natal medical care; or the illiterate who, because of a faulty school system or his own personal limitations, has not learned to function within our society. We must see all of these people as a part of our community. These are the people to whom we have a responsibility. This is the community I refer to—a community without lateral divisions of final significance. Obviously, no Black man can feel secure because of his personal bank balance or other "success" symbols.

So when I speak of survival I do not speak of the continued survival for the "successful," the "talented" and the "manipulators." I mean a social, economic and political civilization in which the "least" of us can live like human beings. Otherwise, what are we all about?

PART III

BLACK STRATEGIES

Chapter 9

A BLACK POLITICAL STRATEGY FOR 1972

by John Conyers, Jr.

CLOSED DOORS

It was in Washington that we held the historic 1971 Congressional Black Caucus dinner. Ever since that dinner we have been trying to put together a plan that could get ourselves together. How do we maximize the power of twenty-four million Black Americans? Now that it becomes clear that politics is the consideration of power, what are we to do? Now that the examples of Irish power in Massachusetts, of Southern power emanating from Bourbon political plantations, and of the machine politics in Chicago have been studied, what have we learned?

Ironically in 1872, when he ran for Vice-President, Frederick Douglass perceived the dilemma of the American two-party system and he proclaimed that the time had come when the principles of eternal justice and human equity should be carried into our legislative halls, our courts and marketplaces. One hundred years later we find ourselves in the same bind. We remain in a political system that is unresponsive to the needs of the people. The truth is particularly apparent when we understand that this lack of responsiveness has brought about an increasing loss of faith in the American political system within the Black community.

When the choice was between a John F. Kennedy and a Richard M. Nixon, it was easy for the Democratic party to take the Black vote for granted. In 1960 Black men, women and children were beaten, cattle-prodded and fire-hosed in the streets of Birmingham, Alabama, by Bull Connor. Their cries could readily be ignored because it was understood that Blacks had no place to go other than the Democratic camp.

When the choice was between Lyndon Johnson and Barry Goldwater, the alternative for Blacks was again obviously predetermined. The Democratic convention of 1964 could and did deny the legitimate claim for recognition by the Mississippi Freedom Party led by Aaron Henry.

When the choice was between Hubert Humphrey and Richard Nixon, the Democratic party did not have to respond to Black demands to gain our support. It could even ignore the Kerner Commission recommendations on civil disorders given to the Johnson Administration when drafting its platform. One might argue that limited gains were made in 1968 by the seating of the Mississippi Freedom Party delegation. Yet it is most significant that the Mississippi challenge has never been fully resolved; the present Democratic Caucus in Congress seated the regular Mississippi Democratic party, allowing members wedded to an openly racist party to retain their committee seniority.

Clearly, meaningful political participation has been continuously closed to most of us. The national Republican party has never been an alternative, and thus the national Democratic party has never wanted to nor has it ever been effectively forced to respond to our needs. The political processes have failed us precisely because the political leadership has failed. With a Congressional Democratic leadership which still supports racist state parties, the road ahead to serious party reform is a long and rocky one, indeed. Unless we elect to be taken for granted once again by the Democratic party, what are the political alternatives for 1972? The only real choices that remain are either to create a political strategy which would maximize our political leverage and open the way for us to form coalitions with other segments of the electorate, join the Republicans, dissociate from electoral politics entirely or begin a fourth party.

A "NATIONAL" STRATEGY

I propose that we draft a candidate to run as the Democratic nominee for President. The candidate, running on a people's platform, would then enter selected statewide primaries between now and July 1972. This would stimulate registration and encourage Black citizens to run for delegate seats to the national convention in larger numbers than ever before. We would then be in a position to exert maximum leverage in the decision-making that would take place in and out of the conventions. Such a strategy might counteract the loss of faith in the political process being voiced by many Black Americans who have come to perceive that our vote has been largely taken for granted. Since many white voters are beginning to express the same reservations, the coalition prospects have a brighter potential for success than at any time in recent memory.

There are several important questions which must be answered in relation to a national strategy. What might be gained by such a strategy? Are there other viable alternatives? Is the strategy limited to running a Black candidate for President in Democratic primaries?

The vast majority of registered Black voters in the country are Democratic, as are the majority of over 1,500 Black elected officials. It is estimated that 85 percent of the Black Americans who voted in the 1968 general elections cast their ballots for the Democratic nominee. To attempt to sway that many people to support a third-party effort in 1972 is a Herculean task that would waste time, effort and other resources.

Secondly, any attempt at formulating a national strategy must, of necessity, be based on coalition politics. In the past we have too often attempted coalitions without having an independent power base. By coalescing Blacks within the party we can solidify and enhance our power base and thus increase our bargaining position.

This does not mean that a national political strategy

will be or should be limited to states where there are preferential primaries. There is much political work to be done in the non-primary states as well.

There is mounting evidence that the McGovern Commission recommendations have not been implemented in a great number of state delegations. As many as forty states are in some degree of non-compliance. We must move with great precision. This challenge must be laid directly before the Credentials Committee and the Democratic National Committee. We will demand more Black representation at the 1972 convention where we traditionally engage in the ritual of selecting a nominee. And not just more Blacks, but more women, more youth, more poor, more representation of every minority. We are willing and ready to tie up the convention and fight for this legitimate representation. We will go into federal courts. We will challenge a convention that does not represent the people. Unless we stand firm on this issue, we are guilty of helping to fool the people into participating in this farce.

The political arena in which the Black politician usually finds himself is inherently anti-Black, whether he represents an urban, rural or surburban district; whether he represents a white district, a Black district or a racially mixed district. This is a reality of politics he can never forget.

The key point about the campaigns of Dick Hatcher in Gary, Indiana, Carl Stokes in Cleveland, Ken Gibson in Newark, Howard Lee in Chapel Hill, Charles Evers in Fayette, Mississippi, and Tom Bradley in Los Angeles is not whether they won or lost or even whether they ran on a pro-Black platform. What each of them did was to accept the immutable thesis that to win political office a candidate must build an effective political organization. Any emerging Black strategy on a national level is going to have to face that same reality.

Beyond that a national strategy is going to have to face the fact that every eligible Black who can be persuaded to do so must register and vote. We are going to have to recognize that it is impossible to campaign without resources and that means some may have to give up more than lunch money.

A BLACK CANDIDATE FOR PRESIDENT

We have already determined that for a Black candidate to be considered serious in his resolve to run for President, it will be incumbent upon him to enter selected Presidential primaries. Currently there are twenty-two states which hold primary elections; of this number there are thirteen states which hold Presidential preference primaries and nine states which hold delegate-selection primaries. A decision as to which state primaries to enter must be based to some degree upon the physical presence of a Black population. This would include such states as Florida, Tennessee, North Carolina and Maryland.

The candidate must be careful not to limit himself only to those states with a large black population, for I do not propose a Black racist strategy. The candidate must be sure to base his campaign around the large concentrations of Blacks found in our urban centers, but he cannot limit himself to these urban areas. The candidate must realize that the majority of Blacks still reside in the South and must campaign vigorously there.

It may be incumbent upon the candidate to hike through the snowy mountains of New Hampshire, to cover the lush dairy land of Wisconsin, to trek the arid expanses of New Mexico and to bask in the golden sunshine of California.

In considering running a candidate for President, one must expect the inevitable query: What do you expect to be the result of running a Black candidate for President? One result may be viewed as absolutely fundamental for the development of any political group: The entire country is now put on notice that we are no longer satisfied being Black leaders but have resolved to take our rightful place as national leaders.

The presence of a Black candidate in the Presidential race will have a profound effect upon three elements of the political community. It will force those people who seek nomination for President to broaden their voter appeal. These candidates will not be able to ignore the concentrated power of a Black national coalition behind a Black Presidential candidate. It will not only force them to recruit Blacks to work as key members of their staffs but also to name Blacks on their delegate slates to the convention. Finally it will cause candidates and those delegations committed to them to support the reforms required by the McGovern-Fraser Commission.

The existence of an aggressive Black national coalition just might cause the Democratic national convention to adopt a platform that is at least more fair to Blacks. It will encourage the convention rigidly to enforce those eighteen guidelines adopted by the Democratic National Committee which are the prerequisites for all state delegations to meet in order to be seated validly. And it will cause the Credentials Committee to inspect scrupulously all delegations to the convention and deny seats to those delegations invalidly selected.

The formulation of a national strategy makes it impossible to exclude the Republican party. Republicans do not even pretend to possess the semblance of serious political reform, as a stony silence pervades on the subject of proportional representation and participation by Blacks, women and young people. The Michigan delegation to the Democratic national convention in 1968 had more Blacks than the entire Republican national convention. Therefore, we must call upon the leading Black Republican in the country—Senator Edward Brooke— to challenge his party in the same manner that we are challenging ours. He must assume the responsibility for initiating reforms within his party or be held answerable to his people, in the same manner that every politician should be called into account.

If it becomes clear that reform of the two major parties will not occur, then the major parties will discover it difficult, if not impossible, to retain Blacks within the traditionally unresponsive two-party system. The existence of a national coalition will inform all other segments of the American electorate that Blacks are an organized and powerful force. We will no longer be satisfied to play a backstage balance-of-power role, when in coalition with other groups we may constitute a viable majority.

Chapter 10

A BLACK
SOUTHERN STRATEGY

by Julian Bond

NECESSITY OF POLITICS

The direction Black and poor people have to take for
the rest of the Seventies is toward a real and more
meaningful participation in politics. That is because it
is politics that decides what kind of life each of us will
have, what kind of world we will live in, what kind of
future—if any at all—our children are going to have.

It was politics that sent our sons and brothers and
uncles and fathers to Southeast Asia to shoot and kill
and be killed by other mothers' sons in a war made by
politicians. It will be politics that brings them back
home. It is politics that decides that unemployment for
Black people will remain two and three times the national average. It is politics that decides that Black people live in a permanent depression. And it is politics

that can put money into our pockets and give us jobs and a livable—not a laughable—income right now.

It is politics that decides that Black people have to live in second- and third-hand homes that other people have discarded, or in vertical prisons of concrete and glass designed by architects who live in the suburbs. It is politics that made it impossible for so many of us to earn a living down South and ran us into the cities up North to be squeezed together like sardines in a can.

It is politics that will enable us to take over the cities where we live and turn them into the kinds of places where everyone wants to live and raise their children. It is politics that gives our children lead poisoning. It is politics that has created socialism for Lockheed Aircraft and welfare capitalism for the poor. It is politics that has made us "the last to be hired and the first to be fired." It is politics that gives our children twelve years of school but only six years of education. It is politics that has made our young men first in war, last in peace and seldom in the hearts of their countrymen. Finally, it is politics that decides whether or not we live or die, whether we rise or fall, whether we work or starve, whether we fight or surrender, or whether we shall have full manhood rights here and now.

POLITICS OF SELF-INTEREST

But the kind of politics that has done these things to us is not the kind of politics that we have to play. Our politics ought to be different and new. That is to say that the kind of politics that has been played on us is not the kind of politics that ought to be played by us. And that doesn't mean that we ought to be soft or say "No" when we want to say "Yes" or laugh when there is nothing funny or scratch when we don't itch. It only means that other people's dirty tricks are not for us. Now, the kind of politics that we have suffered from has been the art of the compromise and the art of the possible. That means and always has meant that unless we compromised, everything was meaningless. But our politics has got to be a new art—the art of saying who gets how much of what from whom. Let me say that again: Our politics ought to be the art of saying who gets how much of what from whom. And quite naturally we are the "who" who have not got anything of anything from "you-know-who."

What is the solution? The solution is that we learn to play this new kind of politics for our own benefit. As we have heard over and over, we have no permanent friends, no permanent enemies, only important interests. Now, none of us forms our own Black political caucuses to jump on one party or to embrace another. We do not get together to beg or to plead or to ask for the impossible but simply to get our thing together. First, we have to divorce ourselves from any illicit dependence on *any* political party. That means that we have to recognize that the difference between the two major parties—the "Democrans" and the "Republicrats"—is little enough. It is issues and interests that ought to motivate us. The time ought to be here in America for politics that would mean we can vote without voting for our own enslavement, that we can cast a vote that would bring us jobs, income, freedom and food and real power in this country's decision-making process. Therefore, the immediate task of America's underclass, particularly between now and the elections of 1972, is to organize. As we leave our caucuses to return to our homes, we have to spread the word that a people together are a strong people, while a people apart will stumble and fall. Hopefully, the United States will choose a new President in 1972. We, as Black people especially, have got to be prepared to have something to say about who he or she will be.

ORGANIZATION AND COMMITMENT

The nicest thing about politics is that no one has to be involved in it if they don't want to. If, for example, Blacks in this country want the people who have been running our business for the last 352 years to keep on doing it, they will be perfectly happy to do it. They love doing it. They enjoy doing it. They get their cookies from doing it. They have gotten fat and sassy and rich from doing it while we have only gotten the kind of fat that comes from not eating enough. Now it is time for us to get sassy, too. These people have been running our business for so long that they think God himself ordained in His heaven for them to do it. But after 352 years of sticking their fingers into other people's pies— here and all over the world—and pulling up all the plums for themselves, they ought to be tired. They certainly ought to be tired of doing it by now. So out of the goodness of our hearts, we ought to get together and give them some rest.

We have to decide—and it is really a very easy decision—whether we want four more years of Nixon-Agnewism, four more years of "five o'clock shadow" and "half past" promises, four more years of the gate-mouth Maryland farmer, or whether we are now ready to get down to the business of putting them out of business. That choice lies only in our ability to organize our poverty and our peoplehood into politics. Now, the best kind of politics for us is democratic politics—and that is with a small "d." That means that we have to secure the right to decide for each and every one of us. It means that we have to make our politics pay as much attention to a street light in a twenty-foot alley as it does to international complications that may turn out the lights all over the world. Our politics has to be a kind of politics that begins on our block or in our kitchen. It is a politics that doesn't begin or end on election day but starts and never ends on the kind of schedule we were used to when we were lucky enough to get a job; a schedule runs from sunup to sundown and from can to can't.

Many of us come from states where party reform is supposed to open at least one of the political parties to the young, the poor, the Blacks and the women. We ought to put this reform to a real test to see whether or not it means us, too. Some of us are from the twenty-odd states where there will be Democratic Presidential primaries in 1972. We ought to get together in these states to run our own candidates in these primaries so that we can be represented at the coming conventions by someone who represents us and not by the hand servants or organized labor or the hand-picked representatives of one of the candidates for President. Some of us come from cities where the racial balance is quickly tipping in our favor. We have to make sure that someone who looks like us gets a piece of the pie that other people have been feeding from for hundreds of years.

A great many of us come from Southern states where there are new Governors. The men are supposed to represent a "New South," but it looks pretty much like the "Old South" to me—the South of Black oppression, the South of cheap labor, the South of cheap politics and the South of cheap prices placed on Black men's lives. A great many of these Governors with toothpaste grins and a new kind of racist populism believe they are going to help decide who the next President will be. If you think they represent some new kind of liberalism, just remember that my Governor, the Honorable Jimmy Carter of Georgia, is the one who asked the Democratic Governor's Conference in Omaha in June first to salute J. Edgar Hoover for his long career of dedicated service, to make the war in Vietnam a non-issue in 1972 and finally to bring the hillbilly Hitler from Alabama, George Wallace, and the racist Governor of Mississippi, John Bell William, back into the Democratic party. If that is the New South, then we are just one step away from slavery.

OUR URGENT BUSINESS

Vice-President Agnew has suggested that some of us ought to imitate African leaders like Jomo Kenyatta. It is significant that he chose a country that fits his politics perfectly, fascist Spain, in which to make these remarks. Well, if he wants us to imitate Jomo Kenyatta and if he wants to continue playing white settler, a lot of us are past the point of wanting to begin playing mau-mau. But none of us ought to believe that the future is rosy. Recently the Census Bureau and the Department of Labor Statistics released figures demonstrating that for every three steps forward the Black people take, we take at least two steps backward. Income for Black people over the last ten years increased, the report said, but our income is still only three-fifths of what white people earn. More Black people than ever are finishing college, the report said, but we are still more likely than white people to drop out of high school. Housing for Black people has improved over the last decade, the report said, but nearly one-half of the rural housing for Black people is still substandard. Life expectancy for Black people is still less than that for white people. But no one has to recite these dreary figures for us. They have been a part of the daily life of too many of us for too many years. The time then has long past for us to begin to "take care of business," to seek political solutions to the political problems that plague us. The important thing, I think, for Black political activists, but for Black politicians like myself especially, to remember is that of all the segments of leadership in the Black community—good and bad, honest and crooked, militant and conservative—we politicians are the only ones elected by the people. We are the only ones that the people can get rid of if they choose. We, therefore, have a sacred trust, a trust that comes from 352 years of struggle and sacrifice by our parents and our parents' parents and their parents before them. It is up to each of us not to let them down.

Chapter 11

BLACK COMMUNICATIONS— BLACK POWER: A NEW STRATEGY FOR BLACK LIBERATION

by Percy Sutton

The borough of Manhattan, in the city of New York, is an island 13.4 miles long and 2.3 miles wide.

It is the home of more than one and a half million people who have their ethnic and national origins in more than seventy nations.

Manhattan is the epitome of urban America. It has splendor, and it has poverty. They exist here side by side.

In the borough of Manhattan, in our people and our problems, we have the widest variety.

I am a Black man and I am the elected president of the borough of Manhattan. In other parts of this country, as the chief elected official, I would be called "Mayor."

BLACK STRATEGIES

From atop the skyscrapers here in Manhattan, one can virtually look out over the backyards, the cities, the villages and the farms of America. I look, and I see cities with overcrowded and dilapidated housing, irrelevant and ineffective schools, polluted skies and waters and streets. I see stoops of slums lined with hundreds upon hundreds of jobless men and women. I see ghettos and reservations in which Blacks, browns, Puerto Ricans and Indians often live out their lives in poverty and powerlessness.

When I look out over America I see Black Americans living in a society that is not of their own making, although the great farms and factories and roads were built with their hands and sweat.

The America at which I look is a militarist America. It is a white middle-class and racist America. It is an America in which several *millions* of people live in abject poverty while several thousands of other people live in what sometimes approaches Byzantine splendor—and it is a white Byzantium.

It is a brutal fact of life that in an America where political power influences economic power, Black people have little political power and even less economic power. Only one in every ten white families is poor. But a full one-third of all Black families live below the poverty level.

Of the more than 1,500,000 citizens residing in Manhattan, only 20 percent, or 302,000, are Black. As an elected public official who is Black and represents an integrated community, I—as other Blacks similarly situated—am an anomaly. For, despite several widely publicized victories in recent mayoral and Congressional elections, Black public officials, of any kind, are few and far between.

Out of the more than 150,000 public officials in the United States, less than 1 percent are Black. An even smaller number—less than one-hundredth of 1 percent —are Black and elected to represent a white majority electorate. This is political poverty standing at the side of economic poverty.

The physical, mental, economic and political brutalization and oppression of Black people in America, over the years, gave rise in the early 1960's to a deep-rooted rebellion in the Black community. In recent years there has been an ever-growing movement toward a "Black Liberation."

However, in all the debates and discussions about Black Liberation and Black Power, one of the most important, and potentially most effective, strategies for acquiring true Black Power has been largely undeveloped—that is, a Black-owned and Black-controlled mass communications system composed of newspapers, magazines, radio, broadcast and cable-television stations.

As one whose eyes have been opened to the power a mass communications system holds and to the good it can do for Black America, I am committed to the development of a Black-owned, Black-controlled mass communications media. I have discussed this matter of a mass communications system with many nationally recognized Black political leaders and friends, and I have met with immediate agreement—and enthusiasm.

The facts are these: In present-day America, information and projection through TV, radio and newspapers is the single most important method for acquiring political office and power.

Political power is won by the amassing of votes. Today, the mass media, in the form of radio, newspaper and TV, is the average voter's principal source of information about political candidates. A political candidate running for any office, above the community or neighborhood level, is what the radio, TV and other news media says he is. His political and public image is developed by these forms of communication, not by a face-to-face, in-person confrontation with the voter.

Until recently, in Black communities and in most urban communities, the prime method of communication with the voter was by the local political organizational structure.

This voter communication method was by an in-person, word-of-mouth method. With a captain and several political workers on a block or area, the now fading, block-by-block political machine had widespread access to, and success with, the voters.

The old political machine also had a high degree of credibility, since those "spreading the word" of the political candidate were usually the neighbor or friend of the voter and were thereby, out of this friendship or sense of personal relationship, able to convince a prospective voter to support or reject a particular political candidate.

There was, too, of course, in the old machine-politics system the ability of the political organization's worker to produce certain visible benefits for the voters, such as jobs, food and favors. Thus, understandably, in this kind of system, the captain and his workers were the people "in the know" on the block.

Unfortunately, with rare exceptions, the old political machine was not a very effective force in the movement for Black Liberation. A fact was that the older Black political leaders who ran, and in some instances still run, "the machine" lacked an economic base to finance their own political campaigns. Hence their funds and their futures were, and are often still, controlled by the "downtown white political leader" who ran the larger political machine.

Without money and without real power to produce meaningful results for the Black voter in the form of jobs, schools, housing and other voter benefits (except with the consent of the downtown white political boss), the local Black machine leader found himself powerless to be independent and move toward real and meaningful Black Liberation.

It was only in recent years, when many Blacks active in the civil-rights arena moved into the political arena and won some measure of control of political machines, from an earlier generation of Black political leaders, that Blacks began to use effectively the local political machines to change their condition.

After eleven years of presenting myself to the voters of Central Harlem for political office virtually every year and being rejected by these voters each year, I, in 1964, won control of political power in a part of Harlem then known as the 11th Assembly District. But upon winning, I discovered that the value of the political machine as a means of reaching and influencing the voters had begun to pass from the scene, just as I finally arrived upon the scene.

The political machine as a means of communication with the voters has a severe disadvantage. It is structured to be effective in reaching people only during election campaigns. Although my own political club and some other progressive political groups are active in the community throughout the year, they are able to reach large numbers of people only during campaigns. There exists, however, in the Black community a desperate need to have political and economic education opportunities made available on a year-round basis.

COMMUNICATIONS AS POWER

It is now clear to me that effective political organization of the Black community will, in addition to present methods, require Black control of the mass communications system going into the Black community.

For a Black person, part of being powerless is the lack of basic knowledge about how the political and economic systems work. Much of the information about the political operation of the economy that the white middle-class child learns just in the process of growing up the poor child and the Black child have no access to. I refer specifically to information such as basic skill training, how to apply for a job, how to prepare for college and how to start and operate a business.

A Black-owned communications media would be in a position to transmit this type of basic political and economic information to the Black community.

WHAT BLACK POLITICIANS ARE SAYING

In terms of educating the Black community for true liberation, a Black-owned communications media could clarify the American economic structure in terms of the system of taxation; the finances of housing construction; the breakdown of budget expenditures for military programs and for social welfare programs; the subsidies for industry and business; and the like.

In short, what Black America needs to acquire real Black political and economic power is a Black-owned, Black-controlled mass communications media of high access and high credibility. What exists now is a white-owned, white-controlled mass communications system with widespread access to the Black community, spreading its ideas, political philosophies and political candidates before a receptive Black audience.

Consider this: There are nearly five million Black homes in the United States, and over 90 percent of them are equipped with at least one television set.

In the average Black home, the television set is turned on for a period of five to eight hours a day. On the average weekday winter evening, close to half of the Black people in America can be found sitting in their homes with their eyes fixed on the TV set.

By the time the average Black child enters school, he has already spent more hours learning about the world from his TV set than he will eventually spend in a college classroom earning a bachelor's degree.

Although Black people have wide access to the receiving end of radio and television, they have only very limited access to the transmitting. That is where the power rests.

Television and radio have not only excluded meaningful Black life from its programming but, except in documentaries and educational TV and radio, have even excluded the lives of poor whites, Puerto Ricans, Indians, Chicanos and other life styles which differ from the mainstream of American life.

Dr. Martin Luther King once said that by lacking sufficient access to television, publications and broad forums, Blacks have had to write their most persuasive essays with the blunt power of marching feet.

The image that is beamed to Black listeners and viewers by white radio and white television is a white image. TV life is a suburban situation comedy lived out in a $100,000 home. Even now, four years after the Kerner Commission report, Black faces in regular programming on the silver screen are rare, and when they appear they are generally in stereotype.

Of course, the old stereotype of the Black man as a subhuman menial has given way to the stereotype of the "supernigger"; but it is a stereotype nonetheless.

How often does the poor Black family, gathered around the TV set, see an accurate reflection of lives like their own—the real-life triumphs and defeats of life on the streets, in schools, in buses, in tenements, in public housing, in welfare offices?

Radio and TV "news" is what a white television assignment editor, who more than likely commutes daily from a home in the suburbs, says is news. When a Black face appears in the news, it is usually in the role of a Black militant in a confrontation or a Black criminal who has been caught.

My criticism of white-controlled television and radio applies equally to white newspapers.

WHAT BLACK POLITICIANS ARE SAYING

Since the Kerner Commission report in 1967, civil-rights organizations have agitated to persuade white newspapers to report the realities of Black life—by widening coverage to include Black people on natural situations—neither Super-Tom nor Super-Militant—and by hiring more Black writers. This is an important effort, but it is only a partial answer to the problem of mass communications within the Black community.

It is important to Blacks and to whites that the lives of Black people be portrayed accurately in the white communications media and that Black people be seen on TV and heard on radio and written of in newspapers often enough so that white America cannot conveniently forget that Black people exist.

It is, I will agree, important to the building of a future integrated society that Black and white people know what each other are like. It is important that Blacks be employed at all levels in the white mass media whether integration or separation is the Black goal.

But it is unrealistic to expect that any white-owned and operated mass communications media will ever devote a significant percentage of its programming and news broadcast time, or printed space, to a proper coverage of the specialized needs of a deprived Black community.

In our capitalist society, the communications media is financed principally through the sale of advertising, and the advertiser has only one goal—to reach the largest number of people who are able to buy his product.

Because of America's unequal distribution of wealth

and income, the audience that most advertisers wish to reach is a white middle-class audience. Knowing this, one understands generally why we can hardly expect that a white-owned and white-controlled mass communications media will ever devote the amount of TV or radio time necessary to meet the specialized needs of the Black community. To do so would seem to be unprofitable. And what seems, in this case, unprofitable seems also unrealistic.

The situation comedy, the western and the game show are all white middle-class fantasies, based on white middle-class self-images. They represent a white middle-class historical vision and white middle-class values. They are designed to sell cars, soaps and deodorants to a white middle-class audience.

THE NEED FOR BLACK CONTROL

The first step in bridging the gap between Blacks and whites, the rich and the poor, the haves and the have-nots in America is how to afford access to those groups which, thus far, by bigotry and prejudice or otherwise, have been excluded from access to the producing and transmitting end of the mass communications media.

This means all groups which have heretofore been excluded—Blacks, Puerto Ricans, Mexican-Americans, Indians, poor whites and women, as well as those with political, social, economic and cultural viewpoints radically different from those held by the majority.

But I direct myself here primarily to the plight of the

Black minority for the purpose of this article. The hour is late.

Blacks must now be afforded the opportunity to originate their own radio and TV programming; do their own reporting and do their own editorializing about their own affairs; and to express to their own people their own opinions of them; the affairs of the nation and the world. This control of their own destiny can happen effectively only when there comes into being a national system of Black mass communications. This means Black-owned and controlled radio stations, broadcast TV, cable-TV stations and newspapers.

Black-owned newspapers, speaking to Black people, have existed ever since the days of slavery, and today most major urban concentrations of Black people can boast of at least one Black weekly newspaper. And Black magazines are burgeoning in numbers and in circulation, and this at a time when many national mass-circulation white magazines are declining in circulation.

The Black printed news media has, historically, served to make Black people visible and known to themselves. When a Black person was born, engaged, graduated from school, married, divorced or died, it was not "news" to white people; and unless the death was violent or the birth scandalous, it was seldom reported as "news" in the white newspaper. It was "news," however, in the Black press.

Traditionally, since the Black man's entry into the political arena, Black newspapers have served as a channel of communication between Black political candidates and office holders and their constituents. Recently Mayor Carl Stokes of Cleveland is reported to have stated that the Cleveland *Call Post,* a Black newspaper, had been the single most important factor in his successful drive to become Mayor of Cleveland.

But as organs of political education and liberation the Black press has had failings as well. Too often it has, in its writings and in its orientation, directed itself toward the Black bourgeoisie, reporting in detail the comings and goings of the Black upper class, while giving less than sufficient attention to the butter-and-egg needs of the majority of Black people—the Black poor.

As with the white press, all too often the emphasis of the Black press has been on that which sells—the sensational. The latest murders and robberies have gotten the big headlines, while the stories reflecting basic Black needs were often either buried on the inner pages or ignored.

Too often the Black press did not think of itself as a conscious agent for social change or as a channel of communication for those active in the movement for Black liberation. Its editorial policy, as well as its news policy, too often highlighted conservative, establishment ideas and activities rather than educating and organizing around ideas which foster change. This was true, though all the while Black publishers knew, or should have known, that a social revolution was necessary to liberate Black people in America.

With all of its failings, however, the Black press has played a vital role, and present-day Black newspapers are playing a much greater role, in the struggle for Black liberation.

BLACK RADIO POTENTIAL

The picture for Black-owned and Black-controlled radio is far more bleak than that of the Black newspaper.

It is true that an increasing number of large American cities have one or more radio stations devoted to programming for Black audiences; but of the approximately 7,500 radio and television stations in the United States and the 180 Black-oriented radio stations, no TV stations are owned by Blacks and less than a baker's dozen of the Black-oriented radio stations are Black-owned.

How well are the more than 170 white-owned, Black-oriented radio stations telling the Black man's story? Not very well!

How much are the white-owned, Black-oriented radio stations allowing the Black man to tell his own story? Not very much!

With but a few outstanding exceptions, white-owned, Black-oriented radio is a wasteland of rhythm-and-blues music, inadequate news, religious programming and exploitative advertising. The amount of public-service or educational programming on Black-oriented radio is negligible. Yet, Black-oriented radio is today the single most powerful mass medium for reaching the Black population of America.

Recent studies reveal that 90 percent of the 17,500,-000 Blacks in our major metropolitan areas are reached by Black-oriented radio. These same studies reveal that nearly two-thirds of Black radio listeners tune into Black-oriented stations more frequently than into white radio.

BLACK STRATEGIES

Future Black-owned and -controlled radio has within it the enormous potential of being the kind of mass communications device that can inform and educate Black people for effective political and economic liberation. Properly used by the Black-liberationist, Black-owned and -controlled radio can inform and influence the Black citizen in his move for true and meaningful Black Power through control of his community organizations and institutions.

Properly used Black-owned and -controlled radio could open up the radio microphone to high-school students to air their grievances; to drug addicts on the street to talk to their fellow addicts about rehabilitation methods and facilities; and to welfare mothers to talk about welfare problems. Black-owned and -controlled radio could broadcast in-depth investigative news reports that alert Black people to their condition and their potential power.

Black-owned and -controlled radio could discuss Black history and Black culture and service a broad variety of Black educational needs. It could inform, inspire and serve as a showcase for new Black entertainers and artists. In short, it could liberate!

Unfortunately, today's white-owned, Black-oriented radio station is not a Black-liberation organ. It is a blaring jukebox.

Now we move to white-owned, white-controlled, white-operated broadcast TV.

On white television, those few Black-produced programs aimed at Black audiences are done under the guise of "public affairs" or "public events" programming and are, in the main, relegated to the Saturday- or Sunday-afternoon "intellectual ghetto" session when the viewing audience, numerically, is at its lowest. Can you imagine any one of the major networks giving an hour of prime time on a weekday night to a Black-controlled program of other than the Uncle Tom type?

If the Black politician or Black leader really expects to gain true political power and meaningful economic strength, he must be able to produce votes for himself and his city, state or national candidate. But the days are gone when the voters were so close to you physically that a political leader could instruct, inform or persuade them by meeting them clustered on street corners, in meeting halls and in churches.

To gain meaningful political and economic power today the Black community must begin to mobilize now for a protracted struggle to own and control a meaningful portion of the radio and TV industry.

FINANCING BLACK COMMUNICATIONS

The standard way of getting to own a radio or television franchise is to go out and buy one. But in order to buy a TV or radio station a person or group of investors must, at this point in time, have hundreds of thousands of dollars in cash, plus a strong enough credit rating to secure a bank or other loan to purchase the available radio or TV station. Purchase price for these vehicles runs from $200,000 for a minor radio station to $3 to $30 million for a TV station.

This heavy financial load is extremely difficult, if not impossible, in most instances, as a means of Black radio or TV ownership. There are very few Black people now who have the cash or an available line of credit sufficient to buy a large and influential radio or TV station.

Originally, in the early days of the radio and TV industry, the radio or television license was awarded by the Federal Communications Commission to a broadcaster for a nominal filing fee. In many instances these same licenses are now worth millions.

White-owned and -controlled TV and radio represent a government-created monopoly value, since under the law a radio frequency, or a television channel, has no monetary value but is a property belonging to the public and is assigned to a broadcaster for three years. Yet, because the number of available places on the radio and television frequencies is limited, a license to use these frequencies is called a broadcast license—a publicly awarded monopoly often worth millions of dollars.

At the time in the early twenties, thirties, and fifties when the present white owners of our nation paid but pennies for their radio and TV licenses, Black people were, by law and practice, excluded from virtually every area of American public life. It was ridiculous in those days to suggest that a Black man be granted a license to own and operate a radio or, later, a television station. Thus a lily-white media monopoly was created.

In New York City the taxicab-riding public that lives in the ghetto and wears a Black-colored skin faced a similar situation of a government-created, white-owned and -controlled monopoly. The New York City–issued taxi licenses were originally awarded, for pennies, to their white owners three and four decades ago. Today these medallions, or licenses, are worth upward of $20,000, effectively barring most Blacks from taxicab-license ownership. These white-owned and mostly white-driven taxicabs then often refused to come into the ghetto. Thus Blacks were without access to licensed taxicab service.

Faced with the need for taxicab service and the refusal of the licensed white taxicabs to come into the community, enterprising Black ghetto dwellers began operation of illegal cars for hire, now popularly called "gypsy" cabs, giving to the ghetto community regular and even cheaper taxicab service.

Creating "gypsy" radio and TV stations would be far more difficult, although it might eventually become necessary if other remedies are not available. The form of "gypsy" radio and TV stations might be offshore or foreign-based "pirate" stations.

Before attempting to develop "gypsy" radio and TV stations, however, Black people should attempt to "use the system"—that is, to use the existing licensing procedures of the Federal Communications Commission (FCC), the authorized licensing agency for radio and TV.

Because Blacks were effectively barred from radio- and TV-station ownership when broadcasting licenses were freely issued by the FCC, Black political leaders should now, with a united voice, demand that the present moratorium on the issuance of new radio and TV licenses be lifted and that radio and television licenses now be issued at virtually zero fees to Black groups seeking to service the Black community. This is called "delayed compensation" or "reparations." It follows the principle known both in law and philosophy as equity.

BLACK STRATEGIES

Our demand on our federal government ought to be that there be issued a quantity of radio and TV licenses to Black owners sufficient to make the Black-owned percentage of radio and television stations in any area equal to the percentage of Blacks living in that area.

Realizing as we do that TV and radio power means political and economic power, the goal of Black mass communications ownership—and control—ought to be given the very highest priority by Black political leaders, the National Association for the Advancement of Colored People, the Urban League, the National Urban Coalition, the now somewhat diminished CORE, the Congressional Black Caucus and the Southern Christian Leadership Conference.

The demand that new radio and TV licenses be now issued to Blacks represents the only meaningful chance of Black acquisition of radio and broadcast TV franchises and power in the near future.

NEW OPPORTUNITIES

In the future, new and elaborate systems of transmission—cable and cableless television—will have the capacity to end the monopoly held by broadcast radio and television license holders. The present cable-TV technology, and the projected use of the laser beam as a cableless transmission route capable of carrying hundreds of TV channels on a narrow beam of light, permits a virtually limitless number of television and radio signals to be carried into every household in every Black community in America. This is exciting, mind-boggling potential economic and political power. This ability to influence the minds and actions of so many Black people staggers the imagination!

Further, it is likely that by the end of this decade the vast majority of homes in America will be hooked onto cable and cableless TV, not only to receive television programming but to have the same wire, or beam, that carries the TV signals also carry the signals necessary to print a newspaper in a home, connect a home information center with a distant computer or teaching machine, or to permit a viewer to shop for his groceries by pushing a button on his home cable-TV receiver.

The TV-cable franchise agreements developed by us here in the borough of Manhattan, in the city of New York, are now models for many being developed around the country. In addition to other things our agreements with the two cable-TV companies in Manhattan provide for a number of "public channels" on which any citizen may produce programming on a first-come, first-served basis.

This kind of city-authorized cable-TV agreement should make it possible to have one or more Black-controlled cable-TV channels operating in every major city in America. Like the earlier events in communication, Blacks have thus far been excluded, by political and economic factors, from ownership of cable-television systems. But all is not lost. It would make for good political judgment for Black political leaders and civil-rights leaders to begin, now, a national education program to advise Black people of this sleeping giant called cable TV. Black political leaders ought to work for

BLACK STRATEGIES

Black ownership of all new cable-television systems serving the Black communities of our nation.

Once Black ownership of newspapers, radio and television has been achieved, there remains yet another question: Where can the money be found to finance the kind of educational, public-affairs, political, and other programming that I have suggested is needed for a true Black Liberation?

Here the answer is not so difficult. It can be done through advertising, the same way in which the white communications media is able to support its white programming.

Recent studies have shown that the Black consumer market is rapidly growing in volume and in sophistication. Blacks now represent a purchasing power of over $40 billion a year. The Black community is a constantly evolving consumer market. It is a market sensitive to changing conditions and current competitive activity. The Black consumer market is a market which is persuaded to prefer goods and services offered through the Black media. Witness, in this regard, the giant growth of the various Johnson Publications: *Ebony, Jet* and *Black World.*

The factors of access and credibility which make a particular communications medium politically effective for a people or a cause happen also to be the same factors that make a communications medium attractive to advertisers. Experience has shown that many product advertisers have no hesitancy at all in paying money for advertising their product on radio or TV which projects radical, and even revolutionary, programming

163

so long as they are able to reach a large audience which has money to spend. The color of money is green to advertisers. For those who wonder how Black people, owning Black radio and Black TV stations, can support their propagandizing toward Black Liberation, the answer is in the Black consumer who supports the white consumer product.

I have tried to sketch for my Black brothers and sisters an outline of a strategy for the development of a Black radio, newspaper and TV communications media as a powerful force toward Black Liberation.

Over the past two years I have tried to move toward what I am preaching and have joined with others in assembling radio and newspaper properties. We are now hoping to organize others, in other parts of the country. If we are successful, American radio, TV and newspapers will no longer be so lily-white. There will be a system of mass communications in which Blacks and other minorities will have the opportunity to tell their own story, to their own people and in their own way, in newspapers, radio and TV media which they own and control.

This, my brothers and sisters, is a movement toward real power—Black Power, Black and audacious power.

Do you see its potential?

Chapter 12

CHALLENGING THE WHITE BOURBON POWER STRUCTURE

by John Logan Cashin

There is no doubt that a ruling class exists in Alabama. They have maintained themselves in politics through one issue—the color of a man's skin. Historically, their rallying cry has been, "Nigger, nigger, nigger, nigger."

This is the tool the Southern power group uses to divide the black and white lower classes, turn one against the other and maintain themselves in power. It's a real neat trick and it has worked generation after generation.

Do you remember that in 1966 Lurleen Wallace won without a runoff? It's true! She beat eleven others without a runoff. But the Number 2 man was Richmond Flowers with 179,000 votes. Almost all of her opponents were Black. Number 3 was the man who was saying Flowers couldn't win. Carl Elliot—with all of the labor money and with all of the "Oreos" behind him—barely had 72,000 votes. We beat him almost three to one.

Now that was a show of power that we did not take advantage of. We couldn't take advantage of it because we were really hamstrung behind the backwash of Lurleen Wallace winning without a runoff. We were pretty well jolted by that. The important thing was that we had demonstrated, at that time, that the Black vote was substantially the largest of the blocs of the loyal Democratic votes in the state of Alabama. Those people voting for George Wallace could not be considered loyalist Democratic voters. We must understand that. The whites in Birmingham who are in control of the Rooster party do not want us to know our own power because, if used properly, Black vote power will weaken their grip on the money—and they love that money!

THE LOVE OF MONEY

"The love of money is the root of all evil." This is one of the more memorable verses in the Good Book that most of us still revere. When one looks objectively at the short but turbulent history of the National Democratic Party of Alabama (NDPA), the observer cannot help but see that its basic orientation is toward serving the needs of people, in stark contrast to the opposing parties in Alabama, both Republican and Rooster Democrat, that are oriented to serve a small but powerful elite aristocracy that uses and worships money as a means and ends of excercising dominion over other people's lives.

BLACK STRATEGIES

Think hard about who the other parties serve. In each case in Alabama, the major parties serve only to maintain the *status quo* in all economic, political, educational and social endeavors. A great web of romanticism has been woven about the genteel monsters of the antebellum South, and the rest of the nation has been fascinated by the unctuous ardor of tradition that is preserved by this web. So much is this so that the inhumanity of these traditions and the relentless and ruthless nature of their present-day apostles has been lost in the sweet smell of magnolia blossoms.

The real history of the antebellum South is one that placed the love of money and material things above everything else. Witness the standard procedure in the slave-breeding farms of the Black Belt. In the name of "improving the product's market value," the white slave-masters actually bred themselves to helpless Black women. *And they sold the children of this forced sexual union, "their own flesh and blood," into slavery!*

Is there any better example of what the genteel heritage of the South *really* is?

We must remember that after a Civil War was fought, one that the North supposedly won, the morality of that victory was sold out less than a dozen years later by Rutherford Birchard Hayes, a Republican who coveted the Presidency so intensely that he returned the supposedly freed slaves to the hands of the same slave-masters in exchange for their corrupt electoral sanction.

This happened in 1876, less than one hundred years ago, and Alabama and the South are still ruled by the grandsons of those inhuman monsters that were successful economically only because their genteel Christian white Southern consciences allowed them to sacrifice their own flesh and blood on the altar of the almighty dollar.

The political opponents of NDPA have striven hard to preserve their power and dominion. In fact, their political expeditionary force controls the U.S. government. This force of evil has fought to stifle and frustrate every piece of legislation that has been proposed to serve the needs of people in favor of the needs of the monsters who exert power through huge sums of money. To them money means power and dominion. They have forgotten that money is a medium of exchange meant to serve mankind, not to enslave it.

The history of NDPA's opponents shows that they once sold their own children for love of money, and there is little in the present to suggest that they have changed in the last hundred years. If we make any overtures to compromise our moral integrity with this historic evil, we are not better than they, and, worse still, we will have sacrificed the last vestige of hope for the ultimate freedom of all mankind on the evil altar of profit, expedience and cowardice.

BLACK LEADERSHIP

The Democratic party today is not fullfilling the critical role of "the party of the minorities" as far as the Black minority goes in the South. The party continues courting "hand in glove" the white Southern power structure. This structure represents the strongest Congressional contingent of "hawkdom," of suppressed voting rights, of segregation and of ultraconservatism in the country. This is, in short, a Bourbon White Southern Aristocracy which is not going to represent the Black man today or tomorrow without a lot of ear-twisting. From the looks of things in the South, one would think that the South had won the Civil War.

The Democrats cannot represent Black people unless they represent the Southern Black man as well as the Northern Black man. Through the Black Congressional Caucus, there has come a good, positive feeling among Black leaders. All of a sudden leaders are saying "We are," not "I am." The Black leaders need this feeling to get going on that ear-twisting and to get the power for change. Without this feeling of unanimity there is no coming together of Blacks. Nor can there be true Black leadership.

The Blacks in Congress, the Black mayors, Black councilmen and Black executives in the party represent this spirit of "We are." Each is representing a constituency of Black people and white people, people demanding a social and political change. Each also represents a certain credibility for the Southern Black man and the Democratic party. These representatives are "in the system" and are fighting for their ideas and their folks back home. If the Democratic party intends to lead the young people, the minorities and the socially oppressed, it cannot contradict itself. In short, the Democrats have got to work for the Black Southerner as well as the white Southerner.

More representation, more strength must be exercised by the Blacks and by the young. These people can and must speak for themselves. Remember the saying,

"Mother, I would rather do it myself"? Well, it still holds true. And it is important. The people in the process are doing a good job, but there must be more "folks" in the system if the system is going to work. The urban North now has a voice by its Black people, but the South is still holding back.

There is something we have not tried in the South. We have not had political leadership without racism. It is time on the scale of things that we have something predicated on love, fellowship and the welfare of one's coexisting human beings.

ECOLOGY—SAVING FACTOR

A racist attitude is entrenched and ingrained in many Southerners, and this is expressed in a lively way in the political system. The ecology issue, strangely enough, may help finally to break the ice. Somebody has to drive the fact home that we must survive on the earth together. Despite differences in skin color or hair texture, we all breathe the same air, we drink the same water— and we are all being poisoned by the same people. Perhaps nothing may bring that home better than the pollution of our environment. This white Bourbon society has a keen insight for learning what people will quietly submit to in order to impose the exact measure of injustice and wrong that can be perpetrated on them. It's not hard to see why the South has long been a feudal province for industrial America. The robber barons of the North use Judases like Wallace to keep exploiting the South.

BLACK STRATEGIES

Eighteen million fish have been killed in Alabama streams in the last six years. And if you should find one alive and catch him, you can't eat him because he's full of mercury.

Guess who polluted those waters and killed your fish and my fish? The answer is uncontrolled industry brought into the state by the Wallace-Cater Act.

If a poor man catches more fish than the limit—and is caught with them—it will cost him a fine of $50 to $250. But not one of these Wallace-Cater industries has been brought to account for the fish they've killed.

NDPA is convinced that the hyprocrisy, hostility and brutality inflicted upon the little people of Alabama can no longer exist; our aim is to destroy it. There are 310,000 black voters in Alabama. We intend to make them ours through use of the system. The ecology issue in Alabama is a major one. In spite of the new racism which many ecologists elsewhere represent, we can use ecology to unite Blacks and whites for mutual self-interest in Alabama.

From my youth the wounds of racism made their mark on me. My life's struggle, since that time, has been to overcome racism in Southern life. Yet it took on a new form when the National Democratic Party of Alabama was founded in 1968.

By citing a few of the rampant and intolerable evils fostered by the Rooster administration, the political party of George C. Wallace, one can readily ascertain the problem faced by those of us who have worked to make the National Democratic Party of Alabama what it is today.

EXPLOITATION

Wallace's strength and power is sunk deep in the red clay of his grassroots admirers. He calls them the little people. But little do they realize that exploitation of their lot has been greatest during their chosen leader's administration.

For instance, if one examines the entire tax budget of the state of Alabama, which we had done by a certified public accountant, it reflects the fact that between 68.5 to 70 percent of the load is carried by four tax-item categories—sales, liquor, gasoline and tobacco. The poor man pays them all. In contrast, our affluent leaders pay property taxes which are less than 8 percent. It is this inequity of tax burden which weighs down wage earners on the lower rungs of the money ladder. None of these taxes were decided by the voters of Alabama: they were all imposed upon the people of the state by rubber-stamp legislatures that were part of George Wallace's juggernaut.

Somebody who makes $20,000 a year can pay a lawyer to scout out the tax law. Meanwhile, the poor white folks—and some Black folks, but mostly white folks—keep on working their backs off, waving the flag and loving George Wallace. When they find out what's really going on, it's going to make Watts look like a Sunday school picnic.

Another aspect of what's really going on is the more than $400 million surplus fund which sits in the state banks collecting 1½ or 2½ percent interest rather than being used for bonded indebtedness. That's one hell of a contrast to the 5 and 6 percent we are paying to borrow. That's one of the chief ways that the poor man in Alabama is being had.

NEW LEADERSHIP—A NEW PARTY

There is nothing wrong with a system that is open to all. It will work, even in Alabama. It's simply the avaricious people who are now in control of it, the Bourbons. When former Greene County Judge James Dennis Hendron was found guilty of both civil and criminal contempt of federal court, the system proved that it could work. The judge is the first official convicted under provisions of the Voting Rights Act of 1965. When he was fined over $10,000 and placed on one year's probation by the three-judge court, it was the first time in many years that any major justice within the political system had been done for Black people in Greene County, Alabama. Now what we would like to do is spread the Greene County spirit all over Alabama and all over the South. Perhaps in some way it ought to spread to many parts of the North and West as well.

Such a spirit was exhibited as early as 1968 in the National Democratic Party of Alabama platform when we pushed for the eighteen-year-old vote, which has come to the fore only recently in the mind of the Rooster and Republican parties.

There is a definite void of enlightened leadership in these times. Nobody could convince me that Richard M. Nixon, the epitome of leadership in America, knows what he is going to do next. It is remarkably stupid to continue his Southern Strategy when it has already become a cropper and its fallacies have been so glaringly demonstrated. It is difficult to tell who is most given to wishful thinking, the Republican National Committee or the Democratic National Committee, for both of them are being led into a trap in 1972. Both of them will be trying to out-Wallace George C. Wallace on his own turf. It just doesn't make sense, especially since it should be clear that many of the white voters in Alabama are intelligent and that Black voters in Alabama are not Toms.

Why the two major national parties would even soil themselves in such an unenlightened manner becomes a mystery at this point. George C. Wallace is a desperate man and will fight to the bitter end to preserve his movement. There has been enough evidence of this fact already demonstrated. Instead of ignoring the Bourbon South and Wallace, who will be forced to campaign extensively in the Deep South and border states to protect his turf, the Nixon Administration and the Democratic National Committee seem to have been hornswaggled into competing for the Southern electoral votes. This is a made-to-order situation for George C. Wallace, since he is going to win the Deep South—and nothing else—anyway.

One could better fathom the naïveté of the Republicans. They seem to be so out of touch with what motivates people other than money and television. But the Democratic National Committee should know better. Hubert Humphrey, in an enlightened moment of reflection back in 1968, could recognize that it was his catering to the white Bourbon South at the Chicago convention that caused him to lose California and Wisconsin and a lot of other states that would not knuckle under to steamroller politics. He ought to be able to advise the Democratic National Committee that they are once again upon the doorstep of disaster by not recognizing the nature of the Trojan horse in their camp. This Trojan horse, filled with corruptors and traitors to the democratic cause, is quite a fancy creature. This magnolia-scented apparition features the most despicable power bloc in the House and Senate of the U.S. government. They are the aristocratic Southern Bourbon gentlemen who are the heirs and protectors of an economy built in the most inhumane and uncivilized way upon the backs of slave labor. This Southern Bourbon aristocracy is a wily cadre that exercises an illegal seniority. Its longevity in office is a direct result of suppression, repression and the corruption of democratic process. Yet both the Republican National Committee and the Democratic National Committee seek to curry their favor, notwithstanding the fact that none of the powerful Southern Senators are able to, or will even try to, deliver their states to either national party ticket if George C. Wallace is in the Presidential race.

A LESSON TO LEARN

The Republican "Southern Strategy" does not deal with George C. Wallace realistically. He is a cunning political animal far beyond the range of their diagnostic tools. Even Robert Vance, the Alabama Rooster party chairman and the current darling of the Democratic

National Committee, emphatically stated in late 1969 that George C. Wallace was not going to run again for Governor of Alabama. This is the type of intelligence both the Republican National Committee and the Democratic National Committee are going to use for guidance in the 1972 Presidential campaign. Indeed, those who cannot remember the past are condemned to repeat it. One may simply ask a now sobered Hubert Horatio Humphrey if he doesn't believe it.

What the two national political parties have that Black political entities do not have is the money to make guaranteed successes out of honest endeavors. Access to the powerful influence of the media is nonexistent. But what is most difficult to see sometimes is the fact that we have something less tangible than money but certainly more convincing. We have on our side the truth. "And you shall know the truth, and the truth shall make you free."

This truth often can be ominous but only to those who have been trying to hide it. Once the truth is known, good things can happen for the little man and for everybody in Alabama. Blacks and whites then will join together to end racism and poverty and bring democracy to Alabama, as was evident when Herndon met his inevitable fate and when Greene County elected a nearly all-Black government, a first for this nation.

Our party does not label itself as Left, Right or Middle. We do not fit into such arbitrary political categories. Our philosophy has its basis in grassroots humanism. People can expect the National Democratic Party of Alabama to work above scandal because we have to set a sterling example. In this way white people—as well as Blacks—will have faith in Black officials.

We are a party "of the people, by the people and for the people." With the help of friends, both Black and white, both North and South, together with our loyal supporters in the state of Alabama we know that we can win. God being our support, we know that we can usher in a new day when the old-line Bourbon aristocracy will no longer dominate our lives.

PART IV

THE POLITICAL SETTING

Chapter 13

THE SOCIAL ARENA
OF BLACK POLITICAL ACTION

by Nathan Wright, Jr.

A WHITE NATION

American politics historically has represented the public life of white Americans.

The advent of various white European immigrant groups upon the political scene has presented some barriers but none of which were formidable. Outsiders, by definition, always upset the *status quo* and so they are resisted. In Boston, in the late 1800's and early 1900's, the Irish had to put up a bitter fight to be accepted in the political arena. Indeed, it was in Massachusetts in 1812 that Governor Eldridge Gerry initiated the device later known as the gerrymander by which one political group could long dominate another unfairly.

Yet the Irish, along with other Roman Catholic groups especially, had an advantage in their numbers, which were swollen both through birth and immigration. Sooner or later these European Roman Catholic groups possessed a numerical majority in the mill towns where they were employed by the less fecund Congregationalist, Unitarian and Episcopalian Republicans. Thus, in spite of the gerrymander and the threat of civil and economic sanctions, the Northeastern Democrats—rooted in a "foreign born" population—eventually came into permanent and dominant political power.

I well remember an occasion in Boston in the late 1940's at the height of a birth-control controversy when the late Richard Cardinal Cushing held a copy of the telephone book above his head. He declared that it held the clue to Roman Catholic dominance in his state. The Archbishop noted that just a few decades before that time, the majority of names in the Boston telephone directory had been conventional old-line American Protestant names. Now the Irish, the Italians, the Polish and others of European Roman Catholic ancestry had come to dominate. They had been able to immigrate freely, but that alone had not done the job. The production of large families had also played its major and continuous part. The Archbishop saw planned parenthood and birth control—now advocated for the poor and disproportionately for Blacks—as an attack upon Roman Catholic power and place. His prescription to his Roman Catholic audience was summed up in the command to procreate!

America has as its prototype, or ideal mold of its citizenry, the white person of Anglo-Saxon lineage and of mildly Protestant values or outlook. As immigrant groups were Americanized, they took on the demeanor of Anglo-Saxon Protestants. The term "Americanization" implies, for example, the acceptance of the so-called Protestant ethic of hard work. Being white persons already, European Roman Catholic and Jewish immigrants could thus hope to blend with the white American landscape and, in many ways, to dominate it. Yet such persons are still viewed as the "foreign born" or their descendants, whether their families have lived in America for only a decade or for several hundred years.

Black Americans, both in their condition as enslaved and free men, have been Anglo-Saxon and Protestant in their outlook. For them, there has never been a choice. Yet at no place in America have Black men been seen in the public eye as "insiders" in the nation's life. The significant deterrent is and has been that Black men could not become white. Throughout New England and in other parts of the country, including the South, there are exciting tales of eminent and isolated Blacks of unusual achievement whom the local folks have embraced and sometimes have worshiped as a kind of idol. Yet their symbolic significance carried no more weight than did the time-honored figure of an Indian which, in an earlier era, marked the site of a barbershop.

America sees itself as a white nation. Thus former President Lyndon Johnson, in announcing the appointment of the Kerner Commission following the civil disturbances of 1967, could gratuitously remind American Blacks as to which race in America was in control.

It is into the public life or politics of a "white nation" that Blacks are seeking to make a great impact today. Blacks will find—and are finding—that numbers and ability for them do not represent the same secure claim to power and political leadership as these same ingredients have done, in uneven ways, for whites who have sought to enter the nation's political, social, economic or religious life. Yet the arena of politics must be entered fully by Blacks if they are to hope to survive and prosper in their American life.

BLACK SURVIVAL

The question of Black survival becomes an increasingly important one as Blacks seek to gain political power. Unless one's constituency survives, a politician's tenure will be terminated in the halls where the details of public life are determined.

Urban renewal and its updated form as Model Cities serve, in a doubtless unconscious way, the same political purpose as the gerrymander. This is not to say that the gerrymander is not still applied in electoral districts, in local zoning ordinances and in public-school boundaries as a means of keeping Blacks on the outside in terms of sharing in the higher benefit levels in American life. Urban renewal and its expression in Model Cities does a far more thorough and devastating job of keeping Blacks both down and out, however, than the gerrymander could ever do. Urban renewal performs its relentless task under the appearance of benefiting the poor.

For those in Black politics, the dangers of urban renewal were seen early in the 1950's as the program came to be called "Negro Removal." Black politicians, organizing their people to register and vote in one election, would often find that most or many of their constituents had moved before the next election and so they would have to reregister in order to vote again. Politically, blacks have been placed upon a perpetual merry-go-round through the urban-renewal process. Without urban renewal's negative political side effects, it is estimated that Blacks would have had political control in Newark—and a dozen other cities like it— by the mid- or late 1960's. Even today, Blacks do not control the City Council in Newark due largely to the fact that urban renewal has made of that city's all-black Central Ward a semi-inhabited desert. Potential voters to register were cut in half by massive housing demolition—with only a few unequivalent replacements—between 1960 and 1970.

So thorough has been the depoliticizing effects of urban renewal that it has been estimated that from 1960 to 1965, when major federal voting rights legislation was being called for and passed, urban renewal depoliticized more blacks in the North than the Voting Rights Act could put on the voting rolls in a decade. Urban renewal is a major agent of black depoliticization. As national and local Black groups plan massive voter registration campaigns, they must be mindful of the potential frustration and of the self-limiting aspects of such an undertaking as are imposed by urban renewal.

An Administration in power may remove the Black cutting edge in national, state and local elections simply by promising and initiating slum clearances or new housing for the poor. Urban renewal removes renewal-area residents from the immediate cite of urban renewal to a site next slated for urban renewal. Those moving from a permanent residence to a temporary residence would tend to be slow to vote. If one is to live in a place only temporarily, there is little investment in voting. Perhaps the major impetus to vote is the protection of one's property. Those who live in a rental area "only temporarily," whether for six months or six years, would not be those most prone to vote. Reregistration for those who have had to experience it is a vexing task and calls for a high sense of self-direction and for a lively faith in the democratic processes. Where these ingredients are lacking—as they often are for understandable reasons in much of the black community—the Black voter-registration path may become a difficult and rocky road.

This is but the visible portion of the iceberg, however, when the Black politician faces squarely the difficulties presented him and his constituents by the urban-renewal process. The major problem with urban renewal, as presently practiced, is its capacity to make people rootless. The removal of people from a home base in which their roots are deeply sunk is known technically as *deracination*. Deracination is a scourge by which the Black community has been ravaged. Yet the danger-ridden syndrome which this disease represents has not been as fully explored as it should be by either Black community leaders or by national and state leadership vitally concerned for the nation's security, fulfillment and internal peace.

The Black politician, to be successful, often finds that he spends the lion's share of his time assisting his constituents with personal problems and that, even in the legislative halls, his proposals are for programs of an ameliorative nature. Through the present urban-renewal process, such a pattern of activity might be expected to increase. This is true primarily because the urban-renewal process makes tent-dwellers of once secure people and holds men, women and children in continual suspense.

Deracinated, or rootless, people tend to have aggravated problems in education, housing, job security and crime control. The community in which the continually displaced central-city dweller lives is one in which new relationships are repeatedly made and quickly shattered. Hence, poor education, for example, is compounded. To learn, students must reach out to others as well as to new ideas. When rewarding relationships are constantly and capriciously broken, through a seemingly ceaseless moving about, the sensitive child soon becomes reluctant to dig in simply to face another abrupt extrication. Soon also those tentacles which reach out for learning are pulled and kept in an inturned world of more secure fantasy or reality replaces the world into which the normal educative processes would have the young minds enter and explore.

Ghetto youth, caught up in the processes of deracination, may not be as dumb or sluggish as they sometimes appear. They may simply be sensitive young spirits who do not wish to face the pain of constantly crushed commitments.

Urban renewal tends to encourage a parasitic personality within the Black community. This is accomplished by changing property owners into instant renters. This is an especial tragedy with older people who may have struggled for years to own a modest central-city home. Along comes urban renewal, offering not a fair replacement price but a so-called "generous valuation" price. Instantaneously, a proud Black—or white—property owner becomes once more a landless tenant. This is particularly demeaning for those at the bottom of the socio-economic ladder who feel trapped on someone else's plantation during the day and now at night cannot retire to a place of one's own, however modest it may be.

Renters put as little as possible into property and seek to get as much out of it as they can. Such an attitude may be aptly characterized as parasitic. Home owners, on the contrary, invest as much as possible in their property, take little out and have a long-range view both of their neighborhoods and of the nation.

On ethical grounds, as well as for the nation's safety, it might be considered basic to the nation's fulfillment that we become a nation of property owners. Certainly public-housing projects could, with far less cost, be cooperatively owned. Such ownership—after initial government construction and financing—would eliminate the evils of income-ceiling imposition, the thrusting out of those who display initiative, and the encouragement of a user complex with its attendant high maintenance and exorbitant policing costs. All public-housing projects, both present and planned, could become resident-owned with little more than administrative fiat, although legislation should be enacted to require it. Urban-renewal legislation should emphasize at least three ingredients if Black politicians are to serve their constituencies best. There must be immediate cooperative or condominium ownership of all properties in renewal areas. There must be housing built on vacated land nearby—there is plenty of it now in our central cities—to serve the housing needs of those whose properties are about to be confiscated. Experiments should be made with 100-year low-interest mortgages, such as are available today in Switzerland.

In order for Blacks to survive and to feel that they are a vital part of this nation, they must occupy land and possess it. Those who own land as freeholders make up a nation's gentry. In a democracy which seeks human fulfillment for all of its citizens, no less worthy a goal than this should be sought for every man. The Black politician may make a case for his potential moderate— or even conservative—temporary ally that economy and the nation's internal peace may be served best by such a course. To do less would mean that the Black politician will find himself on a perpetually self-defeating grind, remedying ills which might have been avoided and building a voting constituency which, by fiat, may be moved capriciously away.

AN OPPORTUNITY STATE

What we need for Blacks to enter fully into the nation's public life is not a welfare state but a nation in which opportunity is secured for all. We must require absolute guarantees for the highest quality of health, education and opportunity.

Welfare—and its attendant program of the guaranteed annual wage—represent floors below which a humane state would not allow any of its citizens to fall.

Yet a floor must never be seen as a worthy end for a just people bent upon developing and releasing the fullest human potential.

So long as the myth is abroad that Blacks want welfare and no more, Black people—and the Black politicians in particular—are in serious trouble, indeed. The Black politician strategically should be working to substitute for the welfare state an opportunity state where government emphasis would be placed upon the creation of opportunity for all. Only incidentally, and temporarily, would relief be a lively concern, although temporary relief might be extended forever. The significant issue here is the starting point. When we begin with welfare as a given, instead of with opportunity, and seek to improve upon it, we shall end up always with a vast body of rationale by which compounded relief costs are justified and the main business of developing and utilizing human potential will be neglected.

Practically every adult within the life of the nation has something positive which he can do for the benefit of others. During World War II we quickly discovered that practically everyone had some kind of useful skill. That quite remarkable realization should have remained with us. When we begin with the assumption that every life may have something worthy or of excellence to contribute to the nation's life, we may add to the gross national product and enrich the quality of the nation's life.

The Black politician might do well in seeking to devise a new system of human rehabilitation to replace the degradingly administered public welfare and to guarantee the fullest opportunities for all. Why are so many

Blacks on relief? Not because they have insufficient skills. They are on relief largely from denial of opportunity simply because of race. But what if opportunities are not readily available to Blacks? Should not there be a strong welfare system to provide for these people's needs? The question here assumes that opportunity will necessarily be denied. The reasonable answer is that if opportunity is denied to Blacks, somehow and in some way, worthy opportunities must be created. While the primary—indeed, overarching—goal is opportunity, relief (for whatever time may be necessary) should be provided. Here the emphasis, however, is upon opportunity.

The nation owes to all its citizens not welfare but opportunity. Welfare must be seen at best as only the interest upon a bad check which the nation has not redeemed. Whenever administered, the public welfare must always be humane and consistent with the innate dignity of all our citizens. We need to look to the expeditious replacement of a colonialist system of so-called public welfare which stigmatizes its recipients, which confuses a public debt with almsgiving and which serves by default to stifle the human spirit.

Consistent with what is said here, there should be a national Cabinet post of Secretary of Health, Education and Opportunity where the development and use of human potential would be the focus of concern. Black politicians should be deeply concerned with some kind of movement in this direction since it is estimated that, according to present welfare trends and employment practices, by the late 1970's more than half of the Black population may be on some kind of relief.

The dangers inherent in such a possibility are staggering. An alienated race of unemployed people supported by a white employed majority would tend to be seen as a useless burden for the nation to bear. An efficiency-minded economy would see such a group as a dysfunctional anomaly. A nation holding fast to the Protestant ethic of hard work would see such life as relatively worthless. While in the amended Constitution of the United States the value of a Black man may be stated as legally "five-fifths of a man," upon the open market and in the public eye there would tend to be a sharp and shameful depreciation. Indeed, with the present patterns of disproportionate Black unemployment and increasing technology, conditions which can be described aptly as pre-genocidal may be fast approaching.

Work needs to be redefined in an age of high technology and of increased possibilities of public or community service. Yet, no matter how work may be defined, Blacks must be in the prevailing working economy, in all branches and at all levels, so that their security is one with the security of all others who comprise the nation's life.

EQUITY, NOT EQUALITY

Of all the well-intentioned but implicitly self-defeating measures with which Black politicians and their constituency (almost as a whole) have been caught up, none is more tragic for the nation's internal tranquility than that of Equal Opportunity programs.

"Equal Opportunity" seems like a thoroughly worthy

goal and to be consistent with the ideals of an egalitarian society. Yet Blacks who, through centuries of low self-esteem, have readily settled for half a loaf have failed to see that equality of opportunity means implicit self-defeat. Many centuries ago Plato spoke of the foolishness of an "equality between equal and unequal alike." He recommended, instead, the principle of equity by which restitution for past wrongs is made and compensatory treatment is accorded as acts of simple justice.

Imagine a driver who, by some untoward circumstance whether conscious or not, gains an inequitable five-mile lead over his opponent in a twenty-mile race, with but five more miles to go. An "equal chance" is afforded to both men by providing them with equal gas, equally good sparks and equally efficient cars. At the end of the race, the car with the previously inequitable lead will still be at least five miles ahead.

Not long ago I visited India, where my mission was to ascertain some of the Indian leaders' perceptions of the powerlessness of the untouchables (or Harijans, as they are now called) in relation to the powerlessness of American Blacks. The major differences between the Indian approach to past inequities and the American approach were quick to note. First, the Indian people accepted the fact that all of the non-Harijan people of India had gained in status or wealth, either directly or indirectly, by the past denial of opportunity to the Harijans. Hence, the Indian starting point was not simply the grudging cessation of past wrongs. Rather, it was seen as a self-evident fact that a gross injustice had been done and that all Indian people were in some measure of debt to the Harijan people.

WHAT BLACK POLITICIANS ARE SAYING

This was, of course, a vastly different stance from that of Americans who, at best, have thought of Black emancipation and freedom from legalized oppression as either a magnanimous concession or an act of simple morality. No concept of debt to Black Americans has even been proposed seriously. Indeed, the literature of the nation's leaders rather suggests the largeness of America's heart in bringing the Black heathen to our shores, in Christianizing them and then allowing them to remain among them as a part of the American people. Hence, in America, there was a century of debate after Emancipation as to whether Blacks should be treated "just as every other citizen." It is at that point that we have arrived in America today.

By contrast, the Indian people, when creating their new Constitution after World War II, adopted immediately the principle of equity and restitution for the Harijans. Indeed, a distinguished Harijan physician chaired the constitutional convention. What were the practical provisions of this first approach as the Indians perceived their duty to be? In the parliamentary assembly one-tenth of all the seats were set aside for Harijans alone. Additionally, any other seats for which any Harijans might wish to stand were open to their competition.

There was, on the Indian people's part, the realization that because of past injustice and tradition these floor-level guarantees were required for elementary equitable justice to prevail. Several years ago, shortly before Mr. Nixon assumed the Presidential office, I sat with him in a small group meeting for nearly fifty minutes. In the course of our give-and-take I suggested to the then President-elect that I would hope that his Administration would replace all equality of opportunity mechanisms with mechanisms dedicated to the achievement of equity. Mr. Nixon, as a lawyer, immediately saw the point and agreed that by equal opportunity Blacks would never get into the American mainstream. "That's why we have had our courts of equity," he explained.

If programs for equality of opportunity were 100 percent successful, it would simply guarantee that in the long haul things would not get considerably worse. Those bereft of opportunity are entitled to, and must require, restitutive or equitable treatment. In the courts of equity, no simple cease-and-desist order is given. Rather, where monetary damages may be ascertained, the court decrees triple damages because of loss of opportunity and because of the personal or professional inconvenience or damages involved.

Black Americans require restitutive treatment if a position of equality or parity is to be achieved. If the goal is equality, then equitable or restitutive treatment is the long-recognized legal path to achieve it. The Indian government's example in jobs and education is also instructive at this point. Portions of all government job categories—at every level—were made available to the Harijans (with the candid recognition that the higher the job level, the more nearly appropriate is "on-the-job" training). In education, free schooling was guaranteed at the lower levels and a disproportionate share of scholarships (for preferential treatment) was provided for higher or continuing education.

WHAT BLACK POLITICIANS ARE SAYING

By contrast, Equal Opportunity in America means hiring of Blacks and whites with little or no compensatory provisions involved or implied. "Open Admissions" provides no opportunity for white America to restore some measure of undue opportunity appropriated by whites to the long-standing detriment of Blacks. Moratoria upon white admissions, employment and upgrading would reasonably be called for on a temporary or periodic basis if simple restitutive justice were to be afforded Black Americans.

During the summer of 1971 I visited one city where Blacks represented 40 percent of the population and comprised nearly 90 percent of the local unemployment. A federal unemployment bill came before the Congress with no provision whatever for equitable employment of Blacks.

The Black politician and the Black social scientist, the Black lawyer, the Black historian, the Black economist and businessman—in short, all areas of expertise within the Black community—must work together to redefine those problems which touch upon Black life in critical and determinative ways. Too long have issues which bear upon Black survival and fulfillment been defined—however lovingly and graciously—in ways which spell only self-defeat and potential disaster for the nation. Blacks have been oppressed in American life. Only the oppressed collectively can define realistically their situation. Upon the oppressed also rests the responsibility of assisting those of goodwill who are by definition still their oppressors to see the self-limiting aspects of the oppressors' position as representatives or

196

wielders of undue power over the lives of others. Whites of goodwill in America have seen only the need to restore to Blacks through equality some measure of the undue privileges upon which whites have unjustly thrived.

A CAPTIVE PEOPLE

In the mid-1960's I wrote an article, seemingly quite revolutionary for those days, entitled "The Colonial Mind and the Urban Condition" (*Renewal*, Fall 1966). I simply took the Encyclopedia Britannica definition of a colony and discovered that it fit perfectly the state of affairs in the Black communities of urban America. In retrospect, the article was prophetic. Since 1965, when the article was written, it has become increasingly clear that Black America represents a people set and held apart civically, economically and politically; denied its civil rights; punished at will; and stigmatized as undeserving of the privilege of being accorded the dignity of free men! That is the definition of a prisoner. Today we are more than a colonized people. We are fast becoming the prisoners of America.

Small wonder then that the majority of men, women and children in prison in America today are Black! Those who react to this awesomely embarrassing situation by chiefly calling for penal improvement or reform miss the primary point. There is no major conscious collusion by law-enforcement and penal authorities against Black people. There is—and has been throughout our national history—a cultural perception of Black people as an alien lump within American life. Indeed, Alexis de Tocqueville noted in the 1830's that Blacks were thought of by whites as belonging to a "community" different from that of the majority of American people, who happened to be white.

Tolerated at best as guests in America, Blacks understandably have been expected to be on their best behavior at all times and to mind their Ps and Qs. A policeman, seeing an alien misbehave, knows that the alien had better behave or risk being asked to leave. He senses that the real Americans have sufficient problems of their own not to want to experience any difficulties whatsoever, or to take any guff, from one who doesn't belong here anyway. We also too readily tend to forget that our local courts are designed, as the U.S. Supreme Court has asserted, to reflect local nuances—that is, to apply the local moral code or mores to the administration of the law. Small wonder that Blacks are reportedly beaten, openly, while judges sit silently by, in San Francisco's courtrooms! It has been but a relatively short time—within my own adult years—that Black lawyers could plead the cases of their own people before the courts and expect anything but mockery from judge, jury or district attorney. Black lawyers had to sit idly by to advise the official white lawyers on fine legal points which might be applied in the Black clients' behalf.

Small wonder, then, that at Attica 85 percent of the prisoners were black! The "residents" or inmates at Attica prison are simply legal representatives of all of Black America who are captive people as a whole. Most of the men of Attica, had they been white, would never have been placed there. Many, if they lived in white suburbia, would never have been arrested. The detaining officer would have taken them directly to their homes for reprimanding or to the local justice of the peace to make arrangements for damages or restitution. There would have been no legal record whatever of default.

While the U.S. Constitution expressly forbids cruel and unusual punishment, Blacks are subjected to the possibility of cruel but not what is unusual punishment for them every day. A Black child in school understands quite quickly that the educational system is designed to replicate society as it exists—meaning, of course, that the Black child is, to use Ellison's phrase, but a miniature *Invisible Man*. It means going to school and trying to learn while denying who you are. All during the 1920's, 30's, 40's, and 50's—and even into the 1960's—I survived, and even excelled, in school largely by denying who I was. I had to enter a white man's world in which I was an alien and pretend that I was white. In my later, adult years I found that I had to engage in the exercise of understanding white teachers and fellow students so that I might someday use what I learned from them against their logic and against the tin-plated inventions which they so often saw as substantive reality. This was to me a cruel punishment. But there was nothing unusual about it, since it was an everyday experience and expectation. It was a part of the fabric of the world in which a Black man in America must live.

It was also cruel, but not unusual, for the Black prisoners at Attica reportedly to be beaten after they surrendered following the revolt, despite the U.S. Constitution, despite a court order and despite the fact that the eyes of the world were focused upon what happened during those tragic and memorable days. It was also cruel, but not unusual, punishment for Black prisoners at San Quentin on the day that George Jackson died reportedly to be hog-tied, hands to feet, and to be placed in the blistering sun for six hours while periodically being picked up in mid-air and dropped, to be cut lightly so that flies would feed upon them and to be beaten with night sticks and burned with cigarettes. What kind of white man's world is this when prison authorities will not "squeal" on one another and when white moral leadership who represent the white establishment condone the outrages in our prisons?

The Black politician is deluged with simply seeking partial relief and minor remedies for only a few of the atrocities which are inflicted upon his constituents. Shortly before the Attica uprising, New York State Representative Arthur Eve was subjected to official ridicule by a legislative investigative committee into prison conditions because he reported that just some of the Black prisoners in one upstate prison might be treated just a bit more fairly. The Black politician can no longer afford the luxury of the individual or remedial approach to a drastic reform or redirection of prison conditions. The prisons are, like the Black communities as a whole, bastions or bastilles of colonialist control, no matter how unconscious may be the combination which is involved.

Community control! This is the basic American tradition. This is the measure of men who are free. The

Black politician, and the entire Black community itself, must insist that whenever Blacks predominate, whites must not dominate any more. Blacks must be in control of Black affairs and of all that pertains to the personal and social well-being of Blacks. This means that Black politicians must lead all Black Americans in the insistence of Black control of Black education, Black communications, all Black-related portions of public utilities, and that an equitable share of all the benefit levels—as well as responsibilities (which we have borne too heavily in some ways and not enough in others)—be the rightful wages of Black Americans.

We as Blacks are, in fact, a community set apart. We must insist that America comport itself as "a nation of many peoples" and that the homogenization of what are essentially heterogeneous elements is not our bag —nor that of many others than ourselves—and that it does not accord with America's peace, well-being or fulfillment. Blacks are not whites, although we are American citizens. We must insist that differences do exist and that our differences in terms of sex, age, race, ethnic identity and in every other way—which does not conflict with the integrity and rights of others—be respected. We must insist that America learns that a nation which cannot respect those whom it sees as "others" is a nation which does not in actuality respect itself.

Blacks must control the police and the courts in their own communities. What Attica should teach us is that Blacks must man and control any and every prison system in which Blacks predominate. Anything less than that violates the essentially American principle of community control.

WHAT BLACK POLITICIANS ARE SAYING

I am—on the basis of principles which I see as essential to Black well-being and our nation's fulfillment—a registered Republican. While I may be slow to vote for many or even most Republicans, I am deeply aware that the verbalized ideals of true American conservatives reflect the programmatic goals of Black Americans. These include broad or massive developmental subsidies in the place of welfare, self-determination, local control, the encouragement of personal dignity, independence and self-sufficiency, the promotion of group autonomy, adherence to the letter of the U.S. Constitution, absolute and even application of law and order, thrift, every man a freeholder, and that the sky is the only limit for ambition, although the sky (with American government subsidies) can even be found to recede.

We need to learn how to make at least temporary alliances, from a Black coalition or third-force base, with people who profess to believe what the Republican party says that it believes. Politics is the art of making temporary alliances which serve a presently perceived self-interest. If our Black political leaders are to free us as a captive and colonialized people, we must make many alliances within the basic framework of agreement that our primary purpose in freeing ourselves in America is to express our collective power and personhood through group loyalty. This means—for every Black man who would see his people free and see America reach upward toward the realization of its high ideals—one essential thing: It means that as a first politically mature step, Black men must, until the Day of Freedom, learn to *vote Black*.

THE POLITICAL SETTING

REHABILITATION AND NATIONAL FULFILLMENT

The American public purpose for its citizens is to facilitate, to enable or to empower all of human life to realize its fullest potential both for its own self-sufficiency and to enrich our common life.

If we begin the political process with this premise, we shall have a different base for defining legislative issues and we shall end up with the most conservative or efficient economy, on the one hand, and the most progressive and secure social system on the other. It is this felicitous combination of efficiency and the good life, shared by all, to which all politicians should and must be committed. The Black politician, as the present exemplar of humane values in our legislative halls, can and must take the leadership in directing the political process toward these goals.

The white politician in America at his best represents what white America presently is at its best. White America is today the leader among the nations of the world in technological advancement and in systems development, the two of which go hand in hand. They have enabled the American people, some of them, to become as wealthy as King Midas and for Americans generally to enjoy more creature comforts than any other people in history. Our technological and business advancement has encouraged scientific exploration and opened up new worlds for all the nations of the earth to enjoy. We are first quantitatively in scientific discovery and we are first at making things and systems work. The white American politician has the awesome trust of legislating in behalf of this interrelated technological, scientific and business complex.

The Black politician does not represent this complex and awesome scheme of things, and this is fortunate for the nation's life. The Black politician, for the nation's good at this particular time, is placed in the position of having simply to stand in the legislative halls representing *people* in their essential human needs. It is, then, the Black politician's unique task and mandate in our day to rehumanize the present system, beginning where he is, in the legislative process.

The Black politician will have to face and to live and give leadership through, what may have become, in retrospect, a largely unnecessary kind of struggle about integration and segregation in regard to our public schools. Here he shall have to re-emphasize that the whole struggle over what ought to have been labeled desegregation alone was—and is—a deeply human problem. The issue should never have been defined in terms of Blacks needing to be in white schools. This is a patronizing and mechanical view of the problem. Blacks are entitled to no more than what all other ethnic groups have had in terms of education in the past and to no less than what they have had. Blacks are entitled to go to school with no artificial barriers restricting their attendance. A so-called "integrated" school, where Black parents must battle for entry, is a gain for the kind of liberal who wants to feel that Blacks need to be with whites, and it represents a symbolic gain for civil rights. Yet completely free and unfettered access to all educational opportunity—fully desegregated quality education —is what Blacks have wanted in essence.

When completely free access is available and when quality opportunity prevails across the board, Blacks may find it to their distinct advantage to be in largely Black schools. If the quality schools of the South had simply been guaranteed across the board and then been desegregated, there may have been only a handful of Blacks choosing to attend largely white-attended schools. Whether many or few so chose, we would not have been faced with the nearly wholesale dismissal or demotion of Black administrators, and much of the present rancor over busing of Blacks and whites to and fro might have been avoided.

If we look at the educational needs of Blacks from a strictly humane point of view, the whole question of public and private schools might be placed in a vastly different perspective. Blacks today may well require privately controlled or privately directed educational facilities in most of our central cities, since our urban schools across the country admittedly have failed. The Free School movement among Black and interracial groups in our cities deserves public support. Wherever private schools are open freely to all the public and produce the highest quality of *educational results,* they should be considered for public support. After all, our schools are designed to produce educational results of high quality. Failing this, their continued public support cannot be justified.

Black politicians—at this critical time for Roman Catholic schools—might well be open to new temporary alliances with Roman Catholic politicians, as Blacks bid for full community control over the educational facilities in their communities. Further, Blacks need to be open to possible alliances with those who would work for full state and national funding for our schools. We need some national standards, especially since adults are coming to live increasingly in communities and states other than where they received their schooling. Education must in the future serve more and more national needs. Why should our local communities pay from a local tax base for what is largely a national service? Our Black communities need this kind of tax relief. Educational budgets in Black communities presently make up most of the public expenditure.

The Black politician can and doubtless should take the leadership in having government provide attractive subsidies for appropriate vocational and academic schooling—in an adult collegiate setting—for those adults who are presently on relief. Dignified options for relief, with irresistible carrots for encouragement, would go farther than anything seriously proposed thus far to get the masses of the poor off the costly relief roles and contribute their talents to improve the nation's life. Our Black legislators might well work with our Black-oriented colleges to plan and fund new patterns of adult education where all in America would have free access —with attractive subsidies where needed—to an education geared to changing technology and enabling them to enjoy their lives in the fullest possible way. With growing leisure, people need to develop the skills and facility to use it wisely. If Blacks are not allowed to work, by reason of discrimination, the nation would be the winner through having Blacks trained to use their enforced leisure well.

In a society which has pressed rugged individualism to its limits, the Black politician is in the best position to give leadership to new legislation which undergirds or safeguards the almost forgotten virtue of interdependence. Children need their grandparents' presence, love and guidance, so that life's continuity, both biologically and in terms of inherited wisdom, is impressed upon our youth. Housing developments which separate youth from age build tragedy for the nation. The Black, Italian and Jewish tradition of the extended family needs to be brought to the center of American life. Geriatrics and child-care centers should be seen as related concerns. In an extended family relationship, further, the question of a mother's emancipation would be placed in a far different light. Women are entitled to freedom, and much, if not most, of it could be accomplished if the artificiality of creating generation gaps would simply cease.

The Black politician comes from a tradition of service and knows perhaps most acutely both the necessity and the rewards of working in an unself-seeking spirit to meet the needs of others. In the place of a volunteer army, which has the real danger of attracting and encouraging the paramilitary mind, Black Congressional leadership might give consideration to a public-service draft in which all youth, at some flexibly convenient point between the ages of eighteen and thirty, might give two years to subsidized public service. An especially attractive option could be for military service, so that those who serve in this way would tend to be representative of all segments of the nation's life. Young men and young women might be required to serve under such a public-service draft. The infirm might not be entirely exempted, as all with an alert mind can contribute something to others and every person needs the sense that he is needed by others. Such a public-service draft could do, in a far more extensive way, what Vista, the Peace Corps and some aspects of the Anti-Poverty Program have feebly sought to do. A new patriotic spirit basically could be fostered.

Black leadership is needed to speak up on the issue of the ecology, which now has much of the aspect of being an adult contingent of a Boy Scout campaign. Our ecological problems reflect at heart the need for a new cooperative, rather than competitive, spirit, in which we invest in and have reverence for life, for persons and for things. The native Americans, our Red brothers, respected the land and the waters. Indian children have difficulty in our schools precisely because they are taught to cooperate and to loathe competition, the motive force behind the American educational system's brand of excellence. We need to learn from our Red brothers, if we are to approach ecology sensibly, without superficial hoopla or acrimony—and even neo-racism—and with the spirit of cooperation, respect or reverence for life which a true ecological concern must represent.

The most pervasive source of malaise within the life of our nation today is the malady of entrenched racism. We are a pro-white nation. Our pathologically pro-white orientation drives us almost psychotically forward toward the conquering of new worlds and the creation of more things *for the future,* since we cannot readily face and live with our sordid past. This is, doubtless, our greatest source of national drive to accomplishment and it could exhaust us prematurely. Because of our feelings about our past, we fail to enjoy yesterday and we cannot feel secure about the present. We live largely by the anticipation of conquering greater worlds. Our entry into and excellence in outer space came thus as no accident of our technology nor as a military or scientific necessity.

When Black politicians speak of a Black man or woman becoming President in 1972 or 1976, they are speaking of a regenerative or redemptive necessity in American life. Unless we immediately change our vision of reality and come to a new perception as to who and what America is, we as a nation may be quickly lost. The maze of problems facing this nation in the late 1900's and early 2000's are far too great for us to have a compass needle gone berserk. We need to straighten out the record now. Several of the men and women mentioned as Black Presidential possibilities are not only electable now but also possess the potential of creating a needed ethnical and patriotic revitalization within the nation. We must take seriously, then, the prospect of a Black man in the White House. A Black woman might cause some men to make a greater reassessment of reality than they might like to make at this present point. Yet it could accomplish much good among us. Perhaps we have had a father figure, weak and strong, long enough. The mother virtues need to be emphasized. Why not now? Or certainly not much later than 1976?

Examples of a growing decadence in our official public life abound at every hand: in our inability to get out

of wantonly wasteful and long-unnecessary farm subsidies while cities languish in need; in relief rolls which
may soon place a minority group in a pre-genocidal
state; in organized crime infecting public life at all levels
and which cannot get its leaders on the "ten most
wanted" list; in the alienation of our youth, who often
turn to drugs to escape the painful prospects of our
common life; in an entrenched educational system which
has only 30 percent efficiency; in wage inequities
which reward power and not accomplishment or service;
and in our escapist mentality, which allows cities to
decay and social, psychological and physical diseases to
plague us while we fight needless foreign wars and, in
moon-gazer fashion, make trips to the moon and plan
others to go beyond it. A preoccupation with the moon
by definition is lunacy. The trips there, in and of themselves, may be relatively harmless. Yet the predisposition
which has driven us there may be no less than pre-
psychosis.

It is in this critical social arena—of grave national
need and of infinite opportunity—that the Black politician with his uniquely saving gifts is called to function
in our nation's life today.

DATE DUE

1/4/11			
GAYLORD			PRINTED IN U.S.A.